THE
NEW GARDEN

An Introduction to the Bahá'í Faith

HU<u>SH</u>MAND FAT<u>H</u>EA'<u>Z</u>AM

Bahá'í Publishing Trust
New Delhi, India

Sixteenth Reprint : November 1999
Revised New Edition : October 2001
Reprints : 2004, 2005

ISBN: 81-85091-55-2

Bahá'í Publishing Trust
F-3/6, Okhla Industrial Area, Phase-1
New Delhi - 110 020, India

Printed at : J. K. Offset & Packaging, New Delhi, Ph. 9810112087

THE
NEW GARDEN

The New Garden is dedicated to the awakening masses of India, as a token of my gratitude for all the good lessons of devotion, sincerity and love that I have learnt from them.

HUSHMAND FATHEA'ZAM

Acknowledgements

The New Garden is based on my revised notes prepared for the Bahá'í Teaching Institute at Indore, Central India. The Hindi version of this book has already been published. As for the English edition, I must offer my grateful thanks to Dr R. Muhájir, Hand of the Cause, who not only encouraged me to prepare these lessons but also enriched them by his wise suggestions and observations so that they may be used, with appropriate modifications, in other countries where the Message of God is being actively spread among their peoples.

In this connection my efforts were greatly facilitated by the generous co-operation of Mrs Gloria Faizi who has patiently gone through the manuscript and has corrected and improved it.

My thanks are also due to the National Spiritual Assembly of the Bahá'ís of India for their approval to publish *The New Garden*.

HUSHMAND FATHEA'ZAM
New Delhi
Riḍván 119 [1963–64]

Contents

God and His Religion

The Purpose of Our Lives

Have you ever compared a jungle with a farm? In the jungle the trees grow wild; there are thick shrubs and untamed creepers. The farm has geometrical borders, tilled earth, a network of canals and streams—a patch of corn here, a field of sugarcane there.

What is the difference between the wild jungle and the farm?

In the farm you can see order in everything while in the jungle there is no *order*. In the farm things have been cared for and tended, while in the jungle everything grows haphazardly and without order.

Where there is *order* there is *purpose*.

We develop a farm for a reason. We dig canals and wells for a reason. We have a purpose in doing all this. If there were no purpose in doing so, we would have left the field to the rains, the winds and the sun. We would have abandoned it to grow into a jungle with all its wild life.

The farm has *order*. The farm has a *purpose*.

Look at Creation as a whole. Do you not see perfect order in everything? Look at the moon, how it comes and how it goes! Next month the crescent of the new moon will again glitter in the sky like a golden dagger. Wait 14 more days and watch the full moon rise in all its beauty like a silver shield. You can count the days of the moon because it comes and goes according to an *order*. Look at the sun, the change of the seasons, the birth of a child, and the growth of a field. Everywhere there is order and therefore there is a purpose behind all these things. They cannot be without a reason.

What is the purpose of our creation? To know God, our Creator, and to worship Him.

If we know God, the purpose of our lives is fulfilled. The purpose of a lamp is to give light. The purpose of a flute is to give out melodious notes. We must know God if the purpose of our lives is to be fulfilled. If we do not know Him, we are like unlit lamps, or silent flutes.

Bahá'u'lláh, the great Manifestation of God for this age, reveals a prayer, saying:

> *"I bear witness, O my God, that Thou hast created me to know Thee and to worship Thee. I testify, at this moment to my powerlessness and to Thy might, to my poverty and to Thy wealth.*
>
> *"There is none other God but Thee, the Help in Peril, the Self-Subsisting."* [1]

Bahá'u'lláh has asked us to recite this prayer at noon *every* day lest we forget why we have been created. Let us be melodious flutes, vibrant with the praise of God. Let us not be silent flutes!

How to Know God

Our life on earth is chiefly dependent on the sun. It gives us light and life. If the blessings of the sun were withdrawn from us, everything would die on the face of the earth. However, it is impossible for us to get very close to the sun, impossible to go directly to it. If we do so, the sun, the same source of light and life, will burn us away. We are too weak to bear the direct heat and light of the powerful sun. But the sun gives its energy, heat,

---

1   Bahá'u'lláh: *Prayers and Meditations by Bahá'u'lláh*, Section CLXXXI, p. 314.

light and life to us through the medium of its rays. The rays of the sun connect us to the sun.

God, the Almighty, the Creator, the Omnipotent, is immeasurably greater than what we can imagine. He is the "Unknowable Essence". How can we reach Him through our efforts? We will burn if we try to get too close to the sun. How can we then ever hope to be able to reach God, the Creator of all things—the All-Glorious, the Most High? We cannot go to Him but He can reach out to us. The sun sends its energies to us through its rays. God's guidance and glory come to us through His Manifestations like Krishna, Christ, Muḥammad and Bahá'u'lláh. The Manifestations of God are the only means that can take us to Him. Had it not been for Them, our world would have remained dark and our lives would indeed have been dead.

If we recognize the Manifestations of God, then we have recognized God. If we deny Them, then we have denied God.

Bahá'u'lláh, the Manifestation of God for our age, tells us:

"The door of the knowledge of the Ancient Being hath ever been, and will continue for ever to be, closed in the face of men. No man's understanding shall ever gain access unto His holy court. As a token of His mercy, however, and as a proof of His loving-kindness, He hath manifested unto men the Day Stars of His divine guidance, the Symbols of His divine unity, and hath ordained the knowledge of these sanctified Beings to be identical with the knowledge of His own Self. Whoso recognizeth them hath recognized God. Whoso hearkeneth to their call, hath hearkened to the Voice of God, and whoso testifieth to the truth of their Revelation, hath testified to the truth of God Himself. ... whoso disbelieveth in them, hath disbelieved in God. Every one of them is the Way of God that connecteth this world with the realms above, and the Standard of His Truth unto every one in the kingdoms of earth and heaven. They are the

Manifestations of God amidst men, the evidences of His Truth, and the signs of His glory. "[1]

The Love of God

The knowledge of the Manifestations of God creates the love of God in our hearts. The love of God is the source of our everlasting happiness. Love is the cause of our creation, as Bahá'u'lláh says:

"O SON OF MAN!

Veiled in My immemorial being and in the ancient eternity of My essence, I knew My love for thee; therefore I created thee, have engraved on thee Mine image and revealed to thee My beauty. "[2]

God created and loved us, because God has loved and will always continue to love us. He will never leave us alone in our helplessness. He manifests Himself to us from time to time.

'Abdu'l-Bahá says:

"Consider to what extent the love of God makes itself manifest. Among the signs of His love which appear in the world are the dawning points of His Manifestations. What an infinite degree of love is reflected by the divine Manifestations towards mankind! For the sake of guiding the people They have willingly forfeited Their lives to resuscitate human hearts. They have accepted the cross. To enable human souls to attain the supreme degree of advancement, They have suffered during Their limited years extreme ordeals and difficulties. ...

"Observe how rarely human souls sacrifice their pleasure or comfort for others; how improbable that a man would offer his eye or suffer himself to be dismembered for the benefit of another. Yet all the divine Manifestations suffered, offered

---

[1] Bahá'u'lláh: *Gleanings from the Writings of Bahá'u'lláh*, Section XXI, pp. 49–50.

[2] Bahá'u'lláh: *The Hidden Words of Bahá'u'lláh*, (Arabic) No. 3.

Their lives and blood, sacrificed Their existence, comfort and all They possessed for the sake of mankind. Therefore consider how much They love. ... Were it not for Their illumination, human souls would not be radiant. How effective is Their love! This is a sign of the love of God; a ray of the Sun of Reality."[1]

God loves us. He wants us to love Him too.

"O Son of the Wondrous Vision!" says Bahá'u'lláh, *"I have breathed within thee a breath of My own Spirit, that thou mayest be My lover. Why hast thou forsaken Me and sought a beloved other than Me?"*[2]

"To be God's lover! That is the sole object of life for the Bahá'í. To have God as his closest companion and most intimate friend, his Peerless Beloved, in Whose Presence is fullness of joy! And to love God means to love everything and everybody, for all are of God. The real Bahá'í will be the perfect lover. He will love everyone with a pure heart, fervently. He will hate no one. He will despise no one, for he will have learnt to see the Face of the Beloved in every face, and to find His traces everywhere. His love will know no limit of sect, nation, class or race."[3]

The love of man for man will be easy if the love of God is in our hearts. In the words of 'Abdu'l-Bahá:

"The love which exists between the hearts of believers is prompted by the ideal of the unity of spirits. This love is attained through the knowledge of God, so that men see the Divine Love reflected in the heart. Each sees in the other the Beauty of God reflected in the soul, and finding this point of similarity, they are attracted to one another in love. This love will make all men the waves of one sea, this love will

---

1 'Abdu'l-Bahá: *The Promulgation of Universal Peace*, pp. 256–57.
2 Bahá'u'lláh: *The Hidden Words of Bahá'u'lláh*, (Arabic) No. 19.
3 J. E. Esselmont: *Bahá'u'lláh and the New Era*, Chapter 5, Section: Love of God, p. 73.

*make them all the stars of one heaven and the fruits of one
tree. This love will bring the realization of true accord, the
foundation of real unity.* "[1]

Remember the Call of God:

"O SON OF BEING!
*Love Me, that I may love thee. If thou lovest Me not, My love
can in no wise reach thee. Know this, O servant.* "[2]

Oneness of Religion

When we are Bahá'ís, we believe in all the religions of the past
are divine in origin. We do not change our religion to become
Bahá'ís because we believe that God has only one religion that
comes to us from time to time. By accepting the religion of all
ages we have made our belief in God more perfect. We have not
in fact changed it. A seed grows roots, then puts forth a stem
and leaves, and later flowers and fruit. The tree is the same tree
all the time. It does not change. It only grows. The sun is the
same sun though it dawns from different horizons. The people
of the world through blind imitations and ignorance worship the
dawning place from which their ancestors saw the Sun of God's
Manifestation. If the same Sun rises from a different dawning-
point, they ignore it and become bewildered. However, when
we look more carefully at the Sun, we recognize it as the same
Sun that has shone before from other horizons.

Bahá'ís believe that all the Prophets of the past are equal in
rank and main purpose. They are all divine Gardeners helping
the growth of the blessed Tree of God. Therefore, Bahá'ís are
united in one common Faith.

Bahá'u'lláh writes:

*"Consider the sun. Were it to say now, 'I am the sun of
yesterday,' it would speak the truth. And should it, bearing*

---

[1]   'Abdu'l-Bahá: *Paris Talks*, pp. 180–81.
[2]   Bahá'u'lláh: *The Hidden Words of Bahá'u'lláh*, (Arabic) No. 5.

the sequence of time in mind, claim to be other than that sun, it still would speak the truth. In like manner, if it be said that all the days are but one and the same, it is correct and true. And if it be said, with respect to their particular names and designations, that they differ, that again is true. For though they are the same, yet one doth recognize in each a separate designation, a specific attribute, a particular character. Conceive accordingly the distinction, variation, and unity characteristic of the various Manifestations of holiness, that thou mayest comprehend the allusions made by the Creator of all names and attributes to the mysteries of distinction and unity, and discover the answer to thy question as to why that everlasting Beauty should have, at sundry times, called Himself by different names and titles."[1]

Again, Bahá'u'lláh assures us that there is no distinction nor difference between the Manifestations of God. Their names may be different but they represent the same Truth, are seated upon the same Throne and enjoy the same nearness to God. He invites us to believe in all of them in these words:

"Beware, O believers in the Unity of God, lest ye be tempted to make any distinction between any of the Manifestations of His Cause, or to discriminate against the signs that have accompanied and proclaimed their Revelation. This indeed is the true meaning of Divine Unity, if ye be of them that apprehend and believe this truth. Be ye assured, moreover, that the works and acts of each and every one of these Manifestations of God, nay whatever pertaineth unto them, and whatsoever they may manifest in the future, are all ordained by God, and are a reflection of His Will and Purpose. Whoso maketh the slightest possible difference between their persons, their words, their messages, their acts

[1] Bahá'u'lláh: *The Kitáb-i-Íqán*, pp. 21–22; and *Gleanings from the Writings of Bahá'u'lláh*, Section XIII, p. 22.

*and manners, hath indeed disbelieved in God, hath
repudiated His signs, and betrayed the Cause of His
Messengers.* "[1]

Religion Repeats Itself

Every year has a number of seasons. The beauty of spring is
followed by summer and then the season of harvest and
abundance. Later winter sets in and nature is stripped of its
abundance and glory. However, the end of each winter is the
beginning of another springtime, to be followed again by the
harvest season.

Every day the morning sun gradually rises until it reaches its
zenith, then gradually goes down again until it sets. As the sun
disappears from the surface of the earth, everything is wrapped
in darkness. All the candles and lamps of the world will fail to
dispel the darkness. However, when the sun rises again—the
same beautiful, the same glorious sun—the darkness rapidly
vanishes. This is exactly what happens with all the world's
great religions.

A New Day of glory sets in when the Sun of Reality rises.
Everywhere there is light. Everyone is happy for the age of
darkness has gone. A New Day begins and gradually draws to
its end. There comes a time in every religion when Truth is
veiled by the appearance of man-made teachings. The more man
forgets the teachings of God, the darker his spiritual life
becomes. When man introduces his own teachings and
interprets religion to suit his selfish motives, an age of darkness
spreads over the world. The only sources of light for us in such
a dark night are a few saints and sages. They are the small
spiritual lights that continue to burn like the small earthen lamps
and candles that shine after the sun has set. Eventually, these
small lights also burn out one after another and the world falls
into the deep slumber of ignorance. This is the time when the

---

1   Bahá'u'lláh: *Gleanings from the Writings of Bahá'u'lláh*, Section XXIV,
pp. 59–60.

Sun of Truth shines forth again. In the past, the Sun of Truth has shone through Krishna, Buddha, Christ, Muḥammad and others. In this dark age, the Sun of Truth shines again through Bahá'u'lláh, the Glory of God. Let us not be satisfied with our earthen lamps and vanishing candles. The sun is shining. Wake up! Wake up!

Bahá'u'lláh proclaims:

"Verily I say, this is the Day in which mankind can behold the Face, and hear the Voice, of the Promised One. The Call of God hath been raised, and the light of His countenance hath been lifted up upon men. It behoveth every man to blot out the trace of every idle word from the tablet of his heart, and to gaze, with an open and unbiased mind, on the signs of His Revelation, the proofs of His Mission, and the tokens of His glory."[1]

Progressive Religion

'Abdu'l-Bahá says:

"From the seed of reality religion has grown into a tree which has put forth leaves and branches, blossoms and fruit. After a time this tree has fallen into a condition of decay. The leaves and blossoms have withered and perished; the tree has become stricken and fruitless. It is not reasonable that man should hold to the old tree, claiming that its life forces are undiminished, its fruit unequalled, its existence eternal. The seed of reality must be sown again in human hearts in order that a new tree may grown therefrom and new divine fruits refresh the world. By this means the nations and peoples now divergent in religion will be brought into unity, imitations will be forsaken, and a universal brotherhood in the reality itself will be established. Warfare and strife will

---

[1] Bahá'u'lláh: *Gleanings from the Writings of Bahá'u'lláh*, Section VII, pp. 10–11; and *The Proclamation of Bahá'u'lláh*, p. 111.

cease among mankind; all will be reconciled as servants of God."[1]

Religion is a spiritual school in which mankind receives divine teachings and progresses in body and soul. The Founder of this school is God. The children of men have to pass through this divine school if they seek progress and happiness. In the beginning, one has to go to the first standard of a school, and there the loving teacher starts with the alphabet and simple lessons. When, through the care and kindness of our teacher, our mind is sufficiently developed, we are sent to the second standard. In the new standard, we find another teacher basing his teachings on what we have already learnt in the previous standard, but adding to them new measures of knowledge. Our mind and body thus grow in this school under the guidance of our teachers.

Can we say that any of these teachers who teach in different standards is better than the others? Can we dislike the teacher of the second standard merely because we happened to love our teacher in the first standard? Can we say that what we were taught in the first standard was better than the lessons in the second standard? Of course not! These different standards belong to the same school. They follow the same method of teaching, but our ages and capacities are different in each standard. When we were six years old, our capacities were very little, so the wise founder of the school advised the teacher of our standard to give us as much knowledge as we could then understand. What we were taught in that standard were the best lessons we could understand at that particular age. If we were given the lessons of the third standard to begin with, we could never make any progress. The same is true with religion. God is One and His institution of Religion is one. It is we who have different capacities in different ages.

Our Divine Teachers, the Manifestations of God, are wise teachers. All of them have one purpose—to help us progress in

---

[1] 'Abdu'l-Bahá: *The Promulgation of Universal Peace*, pp. 141–42.

the Kingdom of God. But man has been developing down the ages and his capacities have changed with his growth. We must therefore see the wisdom of this evolutionary law of progress that God has provided for us through His Manifestations in different ages. We must not allow ourselves to remain in one standard of this divine Institution merely because we love the Teacher Who has taught us in that standard. This is not true love that we have for our Teacher, because if we remain in His class, He will be sad. He wants us to go further and to receive instructions from the Teachers of the following standards too. This does not mean that the knowledge of one Teacher is less than that of another. No! All these Teachers have the same knowledge. All the Teachers are equally wise and important. It is because They are wise, that They give us only as much knowledge as we require at a certain time. They assure us that when we have done our best and followed Their instructions, then we will have another Teacher who will help us to make further progress. Our next Teacher in turn praises the effort and ability of the previous Teacher who gave us His knowledge. In like manner, we see that all the Prophets of God have praised the Manifestations Who came before Them, and have promised further education through a Teacher who is to come after Them.

If any one of us stops his progress in the school of the religion God, he will be a failure. However, if he believes in progress and the wisdom of the Divine Manifestations, then he will try to attain a greater measure of knowledge from the Divine Teacher Who has brought the lessons for this age.

Bahá'u'lláh has taught that the foundation of all religions is one. In all the standards of school, one is taught to be honest, to be truthful, to be kind, etc. These fundamental rules do not change when we move into a higher standard. Whether we are in the first, second or third standard, these heavenly attributes are always praised. They are eternal Truths that are true in every age. These are the foundations. However, the foundation alone is not enough. Something must be built on this foundation that will suit our needs in different ages. This is exactly what the religions of God do. From the same foundation of truth, which is unchangeable, they give the knowledge appropriate to the capacity of man at each stage of his growth. In doing so, they still base their rules on the foundations of knowledge taught by the previous Manifestations of God, just as the algebra taught in the higher standards of a school is based on the elementary arithmetic rules we study in our childhood.

We are now living in a new cycle of human power. This means that we are now living in a new age and we have greater powers and capacities than we have ever had before. Thanks to the Manifestations of the past we have been prepared to receive a greater measure of the knowledge of God through His Mouthpiece for this new age—Bahá'u'lláh.

Bahá'u'lláh teaches us the Oneness of God, the oneness of religion and the oneness of mankind. He has praised all the Prophets of the past and has told us that all of Them have given the glad-tidings that, in the fullness of time, Their beloved Promised One will come. The golden chain of prophethood has been linked through Bahá'u'lláh. It is a beautiful story.

Manifestations of God

Krishna

Krishna was a Messenger of God. His Message was the Message of love. He was born in a prison. This was a sign for us to know that all of us are born in the prison of self—the prison of this world. Krishna miraculously escaped from prison. If we try to be good, if we try to be godly, then we too can escape from the prison of self.

Krishna, like all the other Manifestations of God, was confronted with the forces of evil. He fought against evil and became victorious. No matter how powerful evil might be, the power of truth is always victorious.

Krishna became the king of Dwarka—meaning the small Gate. He was the gate to the knowledge of God Himself. His teachings were for the good of man. But alas! man has rejected them.

Krishna was sad that the people could not understand Him. He complained that people did not believe in Him because He came in human form. They had their own fancies about God and His Manifestation. Therefore, when Krishna claimed that He manifested God, the people rejected Him. This is what Krishna says in the *Gita*:

"The deluded despise Me clad in human body not knowing My higher nature as Lord of all existence."[1]

Even His beloved disciple Arjuna could not understand the Divine Power in Krishna. Arjuna could not believe that the

---

[1]   *Gita* IX, II

temple of man might become the seat of the Divine Being. They say that Krishna had to transfigure Himself into the Divine Form so that Arjuna could see His power and believe in Him.

This means that Krishna helped Arjuna to understand His spiritual majesty and grandeur before Arjuna could find faith in the Lord. The battle of Kurukshetra took a different turn when Arjuna took up arms to obey the Lord.

You know that this battle was the battle between Good and Evil. The Kaurvas, the cousins of the Pandavas, started it. Arjuna, the mighty one among the Pandavas, was led by Krishna to fight the army of Darkness. Krishna was Arjuna's charioteer. However, Arjuna did not want to fight his relatives. His beloved teacher and his friends were in the army of the Kaurvas. Arjuna tried to argue and laid down his mighty bow. But Krishna demanded that Arjuna should surrender to Him and follow Him.

When we find the Manifestation of God and embrace His Faith, we must obey His Commands. This is what Krishna taught us in the *Gita*.

"Surrendering in thought all actions to Me, regarding Me as the Supreme and resorting to Steadfastness in understanding, do thou fix thy thought constantly on Me."[1]

Krishna was the abode of peace. He called us to Himself, saying:

"Abandoning all duties, come to Me alone for Shelter, be not grieved, for I shall release thee from all evils."[2]

Krishna, the Manifestation of God, brought a new civilization. He delivered man from evil and sorrow. He assured His followers that in the future God would again manifest Himself to repeat what Krishna had done. To guide the wandering people of the world to the straight path of God, He said:

---

1   *Gita* XVIII, 57
2   *Gita* XVIII, 66

"Whenever there is a decline of righteousness and rise of unrighteousness, O Bharta (Arjuna); then I send forth Myself for the protection of good, for the destruction of the wicked and for the establishment of righteousness. I come into being from age to age."[1]

We shall see in the following pages how this promise of the Lord has been fulfilled.

Buddha

Buddha was born in the royal family of a Himalayan kingdom. He was still a baby when an old sage, named Asita, visited the palace. Asita was a godly man and he gave the good news to the father of Buddha that his son would become the Saviour of Man.

Buddha was then called Prince Gautama. His father provided his beloved son with all the enjoyments of life. He wanted to make his son a good king. However, Gautama found that worldly pleasures alone were not the cause of comfort. One day He saw an old man, then a man who was sick, and then one who had died. He learnt that all human beings were subject to suffering and death. Therefore He realized that spiritual happiness alone could make all men very happy. He left His home, His wife and child to seek spiritual truth. In the beginning He went to far away jungles and denied Himself food and comfort. This was not helpful. For if the body is weakened, then mental powers also grow weak. It was under a Bodhi Tree in India that Buddha received His enlightenment. From that day He started His great mission to save mankind from suffering. He told men to purify their souls and minds, to avoid greed and dishonesty and to realize that this world of suffering is a place where they should prepare themselves for eternal and spiritual worlds of joy and happiness.

His blessed life set an example for us. While He was sitting under the Tree wrapped in meditation, Mara, the evil one, tried

---

1   *Gita* IV, 7–8

to tempt Him with the wealth of the world and the pleasures of the senses. However, Buddha, the Enlightened One, overcame the forces of evil. His power was the power of the spirit.

Through His wonderful teachings, Buddha helped millions of people of various nations to attain spiritual salvation.

In the days of Buddha, the people of His country were fighting against each other in the name of God. They were devoted to many different gods and goddesses that they had created for themselves. Buddha knew that the way to God was only through His Manifestation. Since He was the Manifestation of God, He did not want people to fight each other in the name of God Whom they could not know except through Him. He was a wise teacher. *To avoid quarrels among the people,* He was mostly silent about God but called upon them to obey Him, the Manifestation of Truth. In this way he succeeded in uniting millions of people who were divided among themselves either in the name of God or in the name of caste. He said, "One does not become a Brahmin by birth, one does not become an outcast by birth. One becomes Brahmin by act, one becomes an outcast by act."

Shortly before His passing away from this earth, Buddha made a great promise to His followers who were afraid that His Cause would gradually die away. He said:

"I am not the first Buddha who came upon earth nor shall I be the last. In due time another Buddha will arise in the world, a holy one, a supremely enlightened one endowed with wisdom in conduct, auspicious, knowing the universe, an incomparable leader of men, a master of angels and mortals. He shall reveal to you the same eternal truths which I have taught you. He will preach to you this religion, glorious in its origin, glorious at the climax, and glorious at the goal, in the spirit and in the letter. He will proclaim a religious life wholly perfect and pure such as I now proclaim.

His disciples will number many thousands while Mine number many hundreds."

This promise gave hope to Buddhists that they would not be left alone on this earth but would receive the light of guidance from another glorious Buddha. Buddha is now rejoicing in His eternal abode because He sees His glorious promise fulfilled in Bahá'u'lláh, the Glory of God.

Moses

In a far-away land there was a group of slaves living a very difficult life. They were called the "Children of Israel" and were working as slaves under the mighty Pharaoh (emperor) of Egypt. These people belonged to another country, now called Israel, but had been forcibly taken away from their homes. Only a Manifestation of God could save them from their suffering. It was Moses who was destined to arise for the salvation of these people. He was alone and the Egyptian Pharaoh appeared to have the power to destroy Him. However, the Manifestation of God is endowed with such a great power that no power on earth can overcome it. Moses, unaided and single-handed, arose to give the glad-tidings of the Kingdom of God to His people.

When Moses declared Himself to be the Manifestation of God, the Children of Israel knew that the time of their suffering was about to end. They followed Him. They returned to Israel, the Holy Land, and started a new life. The Pharaoh of Egypt, with all his might and all his power, could not prevent them. When he and his army tried to do so, they were drowned in the Red Sea.

The words of God transformed the lives of the Children of Israel. Though they had been mere slaves, they established a wealthy kingdom. They became great teachers of mankind. Many philosophers and teachers of other lands derived their knowledge from the followers of Moses. For with His coming, the Manifestation of God not only brings us happiness but also gives us great knowledge and wisdom.

Moses summarized His teachings in ten laws. They are beautiful laws. He told us to love God; never to love anything else more than God; and to love our father and mother and to obey them. He told us not to steal; not to hurt other people; to be pure and clean; and to be always truthful. Moses also made a promise to His people that the Lord of Hosts would in the fullness of time come to deliver them from all their sufferings. He promised that when the Lord of Hosts did come, the Children of Israel would return to the Holy Land after ages of separation, and would be united again in the land of their forefathers.

The Lord of Hosts has come. Bahá'u'lláh has proclaimed that the Day of God, promised in the Holy Books of the past, has come. He gave the glad-tidings to the followers of Moses that their cherished Promise has been fulfilled. Jews of all countries, after an age-long separation, during which time they endured all forms of humiliation and suffering, have now gathered in the Holy Land. They have established a separate homeland for themselves called Israel. According to the Promise of Moses, all this had to be fulfilled when the Lord of Hosts sat on the Throne of judgement on this earth. Many Jews, when they saw how the Children of Israel had gathered in the Holy Land according to the Promise in their Holy Book, understood that the Lord of Hosts had come. Otherwise, it would have been impossible for them to gather in Israel.

In the Bahá'í world community there are many Jews who believe in Bahá'u'lláh as their glorious Promised One.

Zoroaster

The light of divine guidance has always been burning in the temple of men's hearts. Our kind Creator, through His love and mercy, has never left, nor ever will leave us in darkness.

Zoroaster was one of those shining Lamps Who has enlightened the people of a large part of western Asia. He, like Krishna, Buddha and Moses established a new civilization that lasted for centuries.

There is still living in India a small but God-loving and advanced community of the followers of Zoroaster who are called Parsees (Pársís).

According to tradition, Zoroaster was born in the north-western part of the country now called Írán. His parents were of the nobility and he had every comfort at his home that was situated near a beautiful lake. Besides receiving the normal and modest education that was available in those times, Zoroaster also learned to be a good farmer. He learnt in his early years, like Buddha, that this temporary life of ours on this earth, in itself, is not important. Therefore, in the pursuit of truth, He left the comforts of His home and went to a cave on a high mountain to pray and meditate. After ten years, when He was only thirty years old, He returned to His people with the joyful announcement that He was now the Bearer of a message from the Supreme Being, Ahurámazdá. He gave the glad-tidings that there is an eternal life in store for us. He invited the people to observe the three principles of good thought, good deeds and good speech. He considered good and evil to be permanently at war with each other, and said that Ahurámazdá, the Essence of Good, would ultimately destroy Ahríman, the Evil One. He also brought a number of teachings concerning one's daily life and stressed cleanliness of the body, soul and home.

Zoroaster, as all the other Manifestations of God before and after Him, was rejected by His people. In one of His Holy Books, the *Avestá*, He remonstrated, "Where can I go? The leaders and nobility are denouncing Me. Even the farmers have turned against Me. How can I be happy with those, who though bound with falsehoods, are ruling our people, O Mazdá, how can I make You happy?"

He further complained that even His relatives had forsaken Him and that the people persecuted and offended Him. He therefore left His home and went east to Balkh to announce His mission to Gushtásb, the King of that land. As expected, the people there were also reluctant to accept a new religion. They preferred their old ways and traditions and were happier to remain in darkness than to make any effort to see the light. The King, however, was impressed with the courage and sincerity of this Man. He ordered his sages and noblemen to arrange a public debate in his court. The debate made it clear to everybody that the power of Zoroaster was not in Himself but was given to Him by Almighty God. Then the King and his people submitted to the call of Ahurámazdá, and a new Faith emerged.

People of neighbouring countries were alarmed that good was established in the Kingdom of Balkh and that it threatened the evil life they were pursuing. They gathered a great army and attacked the Íránian Kingdom. Zoroaster was captured while He was praying in a temple and at the age of 77 was killed by the sword of a soldier. Thus the life of a Harbinger of Truth ended, but His Mission is everlasting.

Zoroaster is an eternal inextinguishable Fire of the Most Great Spirit. Tradition has it that when He was debating at the King's court, fire appeared from His hands and emitted light and warmth without burning Him physically. This was merely an outward symbol of His power, not to be taken literally. The Fire of the love of God, which is lit by His Manifestations, is eternal and incapable of being extinguished. This is a Fire that guides mankind and brings forth warmth and happiness to their souls instead of burning and destroying them. As a symbol of the Most Great Spirit's eternal Fire, the Zoroastrians always keep a fire burning in their temples, and they are thus often incorrectly thought to be worshippers of fire.

Zoroaster not only completed His Mission, but also gave the glad-tidings that in the fullness of time, the World Saviour, Who He called Sushiyant or Sháh-Bahrám, would appear and triumph over the Evil One. He also specified the date of His appearance, stating that a period of 3,060 years of conflict would continue before Ahríman would be conquered and the era of blessedness and peace would be ushered into the world. This date corresponds to the age when Bahá'u'lláh announced that He was the fulfilment of all the Prophets of the past.

Jesus Christ

The story of Jesus Christ is a very beautiful story. It is a story of the love of God and the love of mankind, and it is the story of a Manifestation of God.

Before Christ revealed His Mission to mankind, there lived a holy man called John the Baptist. We have seen in the story of Buddha how a holy man gave the good news that the Saviour of mankind would soon appear. That is exactly what happened before Christ revealed His Mission. John the Baptist gave the good news to the people of his time that the Messenger of God would come to deliver them from all sorrows. The people of that time did not like to change their ideas; they wished to go on imitating what their forefathers had done for centuries before them. The priests who led the people did not want a Messenger of God to come, because they were afraid that they might lose their position if He came. Therefore, they put John the Baptist in prison and after some time they cut off his head. John was happy to give his life in the path of God.

Jesus Christ was born in a very simple home. Joseph, who was known to be His father, was a carpenter. Jesus was born in the Holy Land, Israel. He was very good and kind to the people even while He was still a young boy working as a carpenter with His father. When He was a young man, He said, "The time has now come for Me to look after the business of my real Heavenly Father."

He went to meditate for many days, then came back to the people to reveal His true mission. He gave the glad-tidings of the Kingdom of God. One day He went to a holy place. This was a centre of pilgrimage and reverence for the Jews, but they had turned it into a business centre. Jesus pulled down their shops and chased them out of the holy place. He said, "This is the House of God. You should not pollute it with your worldly interests." He wanted to show that the Religion of God should not become a source of material gains.

In the days of Jesus Christ there were very many people who were spiritually sick or spiritually dead. He cured them or gave them spiritual life with the power of the Word of God. He soon became very popular. The priests grew jealous because their followers were being attracted by this simple man who was teaching a new way of life for the people. The priests grew very angry when He told them that He was their spiritual King and the One Promised in their Holy Books. They expected their king to be a man with worldly grandeur. Jesus Christ was only a simple man who did not even wear shoes. Nevertheless, He proclaimed that He was the King of Israel. "I am your true King", He said, "I am the Master of the New Kingdom. These worldly Kingdoms are nothing as compared to the everlasting Kingdom of God." However, the Jews did not want to believe Him. They rose against Him and had Him crucified along with two thieves. Even on the Cross, Jesus Christ prayed for the forgiveness of His enemies.

The Jews did not understand the true meaning of their Holy Book. They did not even know that killing the Manifestation of God would not kill His voice, as it was the Voice of God, and it would later be heard in every land.

When Jesus died, many very simple and ordinary people were among those who believed in Him. They had received a new spiritual life by the power of the Word of Christ and had risen out of their graves of ignorance. Although these early disciples of Jesus Christ were humble fishermen, ordinary clerks, farmers and tillers of the soil, they were guided by a Manifestation of God and received new powers through Him. They scattered far and wide throughout the world and spread the good Message of their Master—Jesus Christ. Many of them even gave their lives for the sake of His Cause. Under great hardships and the threat of the sword, they carried His Message to different peoples and cried aloud that the Kingdom of God had been established on earth through Jesus. Though mere fishermen and farmers, they withstood the onslaught of the forces of the whole world. They conquered nation after nation with the Word of God and brought new spiritual life to all who came under their influence. This was the Divine power of Jesus Christ, the Manifestation of God.

Jesus Christ, like Krishna and Moses before Him, assured the people of the world that in the fullness of time He would come again in the glory of His Heavenly Father. He said to the people of His age that He had many more things to say to them but they would not be able to understand them. He promised, however, that another great Messenger would come later to tell them more about God and religion.

Bahá'ís now give the good news to their Christian brothers that Christ has come again in the glory of the Father. This is what Bahá'u'lláh said to the leaders of Christianity, *"Say, Lo! The Father is come, and that which ye were promised in the Kingdom is fulfilled!"*[1]

Muḥammad

There is a land called Arabia. It is mostly desert with very little water and a hot, unfavourable climate. In this difficult land there used to live savage tribes who were always at war with one another. They were so savage and ignorant that they used to bury their living baby daughters just because they were girls, and women were no more than slaves in those days. No matter how cruel those people were, they were still God's children and had to be educated.

Muḥammad, the Prophet of God, was born among the savage tribes of Arabia. Muḥammad was a simple man. As a young man, He was placed in charge of a camel caravan taking loads of goods from Arabia for sale in other lands. Most of the

---

[1] Bahá'u'lláh: *Tablets of Bahá'u'lláh*, p. 11; and *The Proclamation of Bahá'u'lláh*, pp. 84–85.

Manifestations of God were simple people. Even those who, like Buddha, came from higher ranks in life, gave up their princely positions to live simple lives. God wants to show that it is His wealth and His influence that work through His Manifestations rather than Their material possessions. When charged with the spiritual Power of God, even the humblest person becomes victorious over all the material power of the world.

One day when Muḥammad was praying on a hill-top, He received inspiration from God. He had not been to any school. He could not even write His own name,[1] but from that hour the verses of the *Holy Qur'án* were revealed through Him.[2] From then onwards, Muḥammad was no longer a leader of a caravan. He was the Messenger of God. He went to the people with His Message. At first nobody listened to Him. When He insisted that they should stop worshipping the idols they had built, and should believe in the One True God, the people of Arabia rose up against Him. They called Him a madman. They ridiculed Him as a poor poet. However, Muḥammad went about saying, "O people, I am the Messenger of God. I have come to save you and to lead you to the Path of Truth." This was too much for the proud people of Arabia. At first the people had tolerated

---

1   The traditional illiteracy of Muḥammad contrasts with: "The ignorant Muslim scholars then decided to proclaim Muḥammad an illiterate man!" They figured that this would make the Qur'án's extraordinary literary excellence truly miraculous. Muḥammad was a successful merchant. Hence, He would have dealt with numbers every day and would have had to know the alphabet, from one to one–thousand, since at that time the letters of the alphabet were used as numbers. Refer to Dr Rashad Khalifa: *Qur'án, The Final Testament.*
Despite this, Bahá'u'lláh's description of the station of a Manifestation of God means that the knowledge of a great scholar or spiritual giant is still nothing compared to that of the prophets.

2   The first revelation was probably in AD 610 (1,234 yrs). The first public announcement was about AD 613 (1,231 years), and the Islámic calendar starts in AD 622 (1,222 years). (The time span refers to solar years before AD 1844.)

Muḥammad, then they began to persecute Him and His followers. However, after thirteen long years of suffering, Muḥammad was still calling upon them to turn to the One Compassionate God and to follow His Commandments. Why should they put aside their gods, they thought. Besides, they were too busy with their continuous warfare. They finally lost patience with Muḥammad, so they decided to kill Him and His handful of followers. However, the Mission of Muḥammad was not yet fulfilled. He had additional laws to give to the people of His age. So He left His birth place, Mecca, for another town, now called Medina.

The enemies of the Cause of God organized great armies to kill Muḥammad and His band of followers. Muḥammad had to protect the Cause of God and those who had come to believe in God, so He permitted His followers to fight against the savages who wished to destroy them. Thus, in the days of Muḥammad, as in the life time of Krishna, the armies of Light and of Darkness arrayed their forces against each other.

Muḥammad was a Divine Shepherd. He had to protect His innocent flock from the attack of savage wolves. Muḥammad and His followers initially had a difficult time. Many of them were killed while defending themselves against the fierce onslaught of their enemies. However, Muḥammad continually assured them that the Cause of God had always been victorious and would always continue to be so. When the Muslims, His followers, were surrounded by powerful enemies, Muḥammad foretold that mighty empires would soon crumble before them because they were alive with the Spirit of God whereas others were spiritually dead.

This has happened as we all know. The great Persian and Roman empires were defeated by a handful of Arabs whose lives were transformed after they believed in Muḥammad, the Prophet of God, and accepted His Divine Message. The Message of God transformed the lives of millions of other people too as the teachings of Islám spread from India to Spain. During the Age of Islám's golden civilization many different nations were united in one great brotherhood. They offered their daily Prayers to the One God, the Compassionate, the Merciful. They recited the *Holy Qur'án* which prescribes a life of virtue and submission to the Will of the Almighty. Even today millions of people all over the world pray the same prayer and read the same Holy Book. Muḥammad, like all the Manifestations of the past, assured his followers that a great Messenger would come after Him. He said that the Religion of God, which had come down from heaven through Him, would go back to God after the passing of a thousand years. His meaning is that people would forget His teachings during the following one thousand years. However, after that, He said, when no trace of God's Religion was left on earth, a mighty Trumpet sound would be heard—not once but twice—and the people of the world would behold the Face of God Himself.

A Trumpet call refers to the Call of God. The Call of God has already been raised twice in this age as foretold by Muḥammad. The Báb appeared over one thousand two hundred years after the revelation of the Qur'án. Very soon after this, Bahá'u'lláh declared His Mission. It was the Báb Who called men to God and reminded them of God's great Promise.[1] And it was Bahá'u'lláh Who raised up the cry a second time immediately after the Báb, calling upon the children of God to behold His Face?[2]

The Báb

The word 'Báb' means 'Gate'. The Báb was the Gate to a new Kingdom—the Kingdom of God on earth.

The Báb was very young when He told people about the Message that God had given Him. He was only twenty–five years old. A beautiful city in the south of Írán, called Shíráz, was the birth place of the Báb. The people of Írán were

---

[1]   Refer to page 31.
[2]   Refer to page 9.

Muslims. Hence, the names He was given were very common in that country. He was called 'Alí Muḥammad, and was a descendant of the Prophet Muḥammad Himself. The Báb's father died soon after His birth, so He was placed under the care of His maternal uncle. As a child He was sent to a teacher who taught the Qur'án and elementary subjects. However, from His early childhood, the Báb was different from other children. He was always asking difficult questions and then giving the answers Himself in a way that astonished His elders. Often when other children were busy at play, He would be found wrapped in prayer under the shade of a tree or in some other quiet spot.

Later, when the Báb revealed His reality as a Manifestation of God, both His uncle and His teacher believed in Him because they had known Him since His childhood, and seen the differences between Him and other children. His uncle even died as a martyr for the Cause of God revealed through his Nephew, the Báb.

Before the Báb declared His Mission as a Messenger of God, there were two famous teachers who said, that according to the Qur'án and the holy traditions, the Promised One of Islám would soon appear. These two teachers were Shaykh Aḥmad and his chief disciple Siyyid Káẓim. Many people believed what they said because they were holy and very learned men. These people then prepared themselves to receive the Promised One.

When Siyyid Káẓim died, his followers scattered in different directions to find the Promised One. A number of them, under the leadership of a pious and learned young man, called Mullá Husayn, spent 40 days in prayer and fasting, and then travelled to Shíráz.

Their prayers were answered. Near the gate of Shíráz, Mullá Husayn met a radiant young man who had come out to receive him. This young man was none other than the Báb Himself.

He invited Mullá Husayn to His house and there, on the 23 May 1844, the Báb declared Himself as the Promised One.

Mullá Husayn's heart had been drawn towards the Báb from the minute his eyes rested on Him outside the gate of <u>Sh</u>íráz. However, now that his Host made His great announcement, he asked for some proof by which he could know Him as the Promised One. The Báb said that no proof was greater than the divine verses revealed by a Manifestation of God. Then, taking up His pen and paper, He wrote down His first sacred Writing. Though He had not attended any school except for a brief period in His childhood, the Báb, like all the other Manifestations, was endowed with a deep knowledge that was a gift of God. He wrote with great speed and, as He wrote, He chanted the verses in a heavenly, mild voice. Mullá Husayn needed no further proof. With tears in his eyes, he prostrated himself before the Manifestation of God.

Mullá Husayn was the Báb's first disciple. The Báb gave him the title of Bábu'l-Báb which means gate of Gate. That night was the beginning of a new era. The Bahá'í calendar starts from that year.

It was not long before many people came to believe in the Báb. Some met Him, some read His holy Writings, while others recognized Him through dreams and visions.

The Manifestation of God is like the sun. When the sun rises, everybody sees it except those who are fast asleep. Even the sleeping ones must eventually learn that the sun is shining.

The Message of the Báb was first given to the people of Írán. The Muslims of other countries did not yet know that their Promised One had come. Therefore, the Báb journeyed to Mecca, the holiest spot of Islám, when thousands of Muslims from many countries would gather for their pilgrimage. When He reached Mecca, He told them that the object of their adoration had come and that He was their Promised One.

Nobody listened to Him; but the Báb, had completed His announcement.

When the Báb returned to His native land, He was met by a group of soldiers who had come to arrest Him because the fanatical Mullás did not want the new Faith to spread. These Mullás made every effort to put out the Light of God that was burning in the breast of the Blessed Báb. From that day the Báb had to undergo many hardships. His short but brilliant life was mostly spent in prison after He had made His Declaration. Twice He was sent to prisons built on very cold and forbidding mountains. However, no chains nor prisons could ever prevent the Call of God from spreading. While the Báb was in prison, His faithful followers spread His Message throughout the country. During the brief period[1] of the Báb's Ministry, thousands of people gave their lives for His Cause.

The Báb was still young, about 31 years of age, when the religious leaders of Írán decided to kill Him. The Báb knew that He would be martyred in the path of God. He was glad to give His life so that the people of the world might come to understand the purpose of their lives and turn to God and His eternal Kingdom.

The Báb was taken to Tabríz and confined in a house there for three days. The Báb was escorted to the military barracks the day before His martyrdom. On the way, one of the disciples of the Báb, a young man named Muhammad-'Alíy-Zunúzí, rushed forward. He threw himself at the feet of his beloved Master and begged to be permitted to die with Him. The Báb reassured the youth that he would be with Him on the day of the martyrdom. Then Muhammad-'Alíy-i-Zunúzí and two other companions, who had also rushed forward to offer their loyalty, were seized and placed in the same cell of the barracks with the Báb and Siyyid Husayn.

The day of His martyrdom was the 9 July 1850. In the morning, the officer who was in charge of the Báb's execution

---

1   Six years.

came to visit Him in the barracks. The Báb was talking to Siyyid Husayn who was writing down His last instructions. The officer interrupted the Báb and told Him that the time had come for His execution and soldiers were ready in the city square to carry out the orders. The Báb said that He had to finish His conversation with Siyyid Husayn. He said that no power on earth could harm Him until He had completed His Mission in this world and had finished what He intended to say. However, the officer ignored the Báb and asked Siyyid Husayn to follow him.

In the barracks square where the soldiers were waiting to shoot the Báb, a great crowd had gathered. They all watched while the Báb, and His young disciple, were tied in such a way that the head of the disciple rested on the chest of his Beloved. Then came the great moment. Drums were beaten and trumpets were sounded. As the sound of the trumpets died away, the terrible order was heard: "Fire". Hundreds of soldiers took aim and fired their guns. A huge cloud of smoke spread through the whole place. The smell of gunpowder filled the air. After some time when the smoke cleared, there came a great surprise. There was no trace of the Báb, while His faithful disciple was standing there unharmed. No one knew what to think. Many people said that a miracle had happened and that the Báb had gone up to Heaven. The firing squad and their commander had never seen such an extraordinary thing happen before. Officers were sent in every direction to search for the Báb. The same officer who had brought the Báb, from the prison cell now found Him sitting calmly at the same place, finishing His conversation that had been rudely interrupted. The Báb turned to the officer and smiled saying that His Mission on earth was now completed, and that He was ready to sacrifice His life to prove the truth of His Mission.

The Báb was again taken in to the square, but the commander of the firing squad refused to have anything to do with His execution. He took his soldiers out of the square and swore that nothing would make him take the life of such an innocent and saintly youth. Another company of soldiers was found to carry out the execution, and this time hundreds of bullets riddled the bodies of the Báb and His faithful disciple. His beautiful face, which was not scarred by the bullets, still bore a lovely smile showing the peace and happiness of One who had given His life to proclaim the beginning of a new era for mankind.

The Báb was a great Manifestation of God. He said in His Writings, that the main purpose of His coming was to give the glad-tidings that very soon the Promised One of all ages would appear. He warned His followers to beware lest they failed to recognize "Him Whom God will make manifest." He said that they should lay aside everything else and follow Him when they heard His Message. The Báb wrote many prayers beseeching God that His own life might be accepted as a sacrifice to the Beloved of His heart, the One "Whom God will make manifest." He even referred in His Writings to the Revelation of Bahá'u'lláh, and said: *"Well is it with him who fixeth his gaze upon the Order of Bahá'u'lláh, and rendereth thanks unto his Lord. For He will assuredly be made manifest. God hath indeed irrevocably ordained it in the Bayán."*[1]

The Báb's prayers were answered and His promise was fulfilled. Nineteen years after His Mission, Bahá'u'lláh openly declared that He was the Promised One Whose coming had been foretold by all the Manifestations of God in past ages.

Bahá'u'lláh

On 21 April 1863, Bahá'u'lláh proclaimed to the world that *"The Revelation which, from time immemorial, hath been acclaimed as the Purpose and Promise of all the Prophets of God, and the most cherished Desire of His Messengers, hath now ... been revealed unto men."*[2]

---

1   The Báb quoted in: Bahá'u'lláh, *The Kitáb-i-Aqdas*: Notes No. 189, p. 247; and Shoghi Effendi, *God Passes By*, pp. 25, 324–25.

2   Bahá'u'lláh: *Gleanings from the Writings of Bahá'u'lláh*, Section III, p. 5.

When Bahá'u'lláh made this wonderful announcement, He was a prisoner at the hands of two powerful monarchs, and He was being exiled to Acre ('Akká) in Palestine, "*the most desolate of the cities of the World*".[1]

About forty-six years before this announcement, Bahá'u'lláh was born in the house of a distinguished Minister of the royal court of Írán. From the days of His childhood everybody observed that Bahá'u'lláh was different from other children, but no one knew that this wonderful Boy was soon to change the whole destiny of mankind. When He was 14 years old, Bahá'u'lláh was already famous in the court for His learning and wisdom. He was 22 years of age when His father died. The government wished Him to take over the position His father had occupied. They thought this gifted young man would make a very good minister, but Bahá'u'lláh had no intention of wasting His time in the management of worldly affairs. Being a man of God, He took no interest in the royal life that was offered to Him. He left the court and its ministers so that He could follow the path set for Him by the Almighty.

When the Báb, declared His Mission, Bahá'u'lláh was 27 years old. He immediately accepted the Báb as the Manifestation of God and soon became one of His most powerful and famous followers.

At the time when the Government and fanatical Mullás persecuted the followers of the Báb, Bahá'u'lláh was not spared in any way. He was twice imprisoned, and once He was beaten so severely with whips and canes that the soles of His feet started bleeding. Nine years after the Báb's Declaration, Bahá'u'lláh was thrown into a dark dungeon. This was a terrible underground room that had no window nor other opening except the door through which they entered. In this dungeon Bahá'u'lláh was imprisoned with about 150 murderers, highway

---

[1] 'Abdu'l-Bahá: *A Traveler's Narrative*, p. 80; and Shoghi Effendi: *God Passes By*, p. 186.

robbers and other hardened criminals. The chains that were put round His neck were so heavy that He could not lift up His head. He spent four terrible months of suffering here, yet it was in this dungeon that the Glory of God filled His soul. He writes that one night in a dream He heard the following words vibrating from all sides:

> *"Verily, We shall render Thee victorious by Thyself and by Thy Pen."*[1]

Bahá'u'lláh endured all these hardships for our sake and for the sake of generations to come. He bore chains round His blessed neck to free us from the chains and fetters of prejudice, bigotry and enmity.

Finally, Bahá'u'lláh and His family were deprived of all their ancestral riches and ordered to leave the country. They were exiled to Baghdád in the bitter cold of winter. The road lay along mountainous parts of Írán where thick snow and ice covered the ground. Bahá'u'lláh, His wife and young children, had to walk hundreds of miles to their destination. The lack of suitable clothing made the journey even more difficult to endure. At last they reached Baghdád but Bahá'u'lláh's sufferings did not end in that city. Had Bahá'u'lláh been afraid of hardships and difficulties, He could have chosen to enjoy a luxurious life in the court of the Sháh (king) of Írán. Instead, He was prepared to endure any amount of suffering in the path of God.

The fame of Bahá'u'lláh soon spread throughout Baghdád and the other cities of 'Iráq, and many people came to the door of this exiled Prisoner to receive His blessings. The followers of the Báb gathered round Him from different parts of Írán and 'Iráq to seek guidance and inspiration. However, there were some who became jealous of His fame. Among them was His own half-brother Mírzá Yaḥyá, who was living under Bahá'u'lláh's loving care and guidance. Yaḥyá thought that, because he was respected by the followers of the Báb, he might

---

1   Bahá'u'lláh: *Epistle to the Son of the Wolf*, p. 21.

be accepted as their leader if he should denounce Bahá'u'lláh. He did not realize that he was causing his own doom by turning against the Manifestation of God. For when a Manifestation appears, only those who accept His station can hope for true greatness. Even His closest relatives are not excluded, because a Manifestation of God stands apart from all other human beings and has a station that no one else can share. All the past Manifestations have had brothers and sisters or other relatives, but even their names have now been forgotten.

Yaḥyá's plotting caused disunity among the followers of the Báb, and this made Bahá'u'lláh very sad. One night without telling anybody, He left His home and went into the mountains of Kurdistán. He spent two years of secluded life in these mountains giving all His time to prayer and meditation. He stayed in a small cave and lived on very simple food. Nobody knew His name. Nobody knew where He had come from. Soon, however, like a moon in a dark night, His light spread over all Kurdistán and everybody heard of the "Nameless One". All this time His family and friends in Baghdád, who were heartbroken by His departure, did not know where He was. Then they too heard about the "Nameless One", the great Saint, who was known to have inherent knowledge bestowed upon Him by God. 'Abdu'l-Bahá, Bahá'u'lláh's son, immediately knew that this could be no one but His beloved Father. He sent letters and a special messenger entreating Him to return because not only His own family but all the followers of the Báb were suffering from His absence.

Thus, after spending two years in prayer and meditation, Bahá'u'lláh returned to Baghdád and with Him returned the joy of all the Báb's followers. The only people who were angry about His return were the fanatical Mullás and His treacherous and jealous brother Yaḥyá. The Mullás did not want Bahá'u'lláh to stay in Baghdád. This was partly because He was too close to a number of sacred places belonging to the Muslims, and pilgrims who came to visit these places were often attracted by Bahá'u'lláh's charm and personality. These Mullás kept complaining until the Government of Írán combined with the authorities of the Turkish Empire to remove Bahá'u'lláh to a more distant place—Istanbul. The same sequence of events occurred in Istanbul since it was also the seat of the Muslim Caliphs. Bahá'u'lláh's great wisdom and personal charm attracted many people. "He must not stay in Istanbul any longer," said the fanatical Mullás. Hence, again, He was sent to a smaller town, Adrianople. From there He was again exiled, but this time to 'Akká (Acre) in the Holy Land, which was then a special penal colony reserved for murderers, thieves and highway robbers sentenced to life imprisonment. It was a terrible place and for the first few days after their arrival even water was denied to Bahá'u'lláh, His family and friends. The hardships and sufferings of Bahá'u'lláh in 'Akká are too numerous to describe. In the beginning He was imprisoned in a lonely cell where even His children were not permitted to see Him. He lacked every means of comfort, and was surrounded by enemies day and night. Yet it was from 'Akká that He sent His famous letters to the most powerful kings and rulers of His day. He called upon them to listen to the Message of God and to obey the Commandments of the King of kings. No one but a Manifestation of God could dare to address those who had imprisoned Him, as a king addresses his vassals.

Bahá'u'lláh raised the banner of universal peace and brotherhood from His prison walls. Although the powers of the world combined their forces against Him, He was victorious over them all as God had promised Him in His dream. The Message of Bahá'u'lláh influenced the hearts of thousands of people and many of them gave their lives for His Cause. Through the power of the Word of God and the sacrifices of the followers of Bahá'u'lláh, hundreds of thousands of people, who were once divided under various names, have now become like members of one family.

Bahá'u'lláh was sent to 'Akká (Acre) as a prisoner for life. However, the attitude of the government officials and His jailers gradually changed so much over the nine years after His arrival that an influential citizen finally begged Him to leave that fortress city. By this time, His great personal charm had made such friends of all those around Him—even His hard-hearted jailer—that no one objected to His leaving His prison. Bahá'u'lláh spent the remaining years of His life in a place outside the city of Acre ('Akká) where He passed away to His heavenly Kingdom on 29 May 1892.

The Message of Bahá'u'lláh spread to different parts of the world from the Holy Land as had been foretold in the sacred Books of the past. In Buddhist Scriptures the Holy Land is referred to as a Paradise in the West, the Seat of the Promised One—Amitabha. To the Jews it is "The Promised Land" from where the Law of God will again go out into the world. Christians and Muslims too have wonderful prophecies about this sacred country that has been their Holy Land for many centuries. Since the exiling of Bahá'u'lláh to 'Akká, the Holy Land of the religions of the past has become the World Centre of the Bahá'í Faith.

Bahá'u'lláh is that Great Manifestation of God Whose coming all the Manifestations of the past have foretold. The divine religions of all ages lead in the same direction and teach the same goal—the Bahá'í Faith. They are like many rivers that flow into the ocean. Each river irrigates thousands of acres of land, but no single river is, by itself, as vast and powerful as the mighty ocean because the ocean is the meeting place of all these rivers. In the Bahá'í community, followers of all religions have come together and become united. Even though they are from the four corners of the earth, they have now joined hands in one great Brotherhood, one common Faith.

The waters of different Rivers merge into one indeed, when they pour into the Mighty Ocean!

The Covenant

'Abdu'l-Bahá

Bahá'u'lláh was a Divine Architect. He drafted the magnificent Plan for the unity of mankind. He laid the firm foundation of this sacred Edifice and selected the necessary materials.

However, who was to erect this wonderful Edifice after Bahá'u'lláh had left us? It is true that His plan was complete but even a perfect plan must be left in the hands of a qualified person or the construction may collapse. No matter how perfect the plan and how firm is the foundation of a building, if the construction of it is not properly supervised by a capable man, the resulting building may be entirely different from the plan intended by the architect.

When Bahá'u'lláh passed away, He left the execution of His Divine Plan in the hands of His son. He appointed 'Abdu'l-Bahá as the Centre of His Covenant and asked His followers to turn to Him for guidance.

The name "'Abdu'l-Bahá" means the servant of Bahá. 'Abdu'l-Bahá was the eldest son of Bahá'u'lláh, and was born on the 23 May 1844—the very same night that the Báb declared His Mission. A blessed son was born to a blessed house at a blessed hour.

'Abdu'l-Bahá was only eight years of age when Bahá'u'lláh was thrown into that terrible dungeon in Tihrán. From early childhood He willingly shared all the sufferings of His beloved Father. He accompanied Bahá'u'lláh on the difficult journey from Tihrán to Baghdád, and spent forty years of His life in prison and in exile. 'Abdu'l-Bahá was an old man when He was set free at last. However, the love of God had kept Him happy even in the darkest hours of His life. He had a deep spiritual happiness that the worst of prisons could not take away. 'Abdu'l-Bahá wanted us to enjoy that kind of happiness, too. He says:

> *"Happiness consists of two kinds; physical and spiritual. The physical happiness is limited; its utmost duration is one day, one month, one year. It hath no result. Spiritual happiness is eternal and unfathomable. This kind of happiness appeareth in one's soul with the love of God and suffereth one to attain to the virtues and perfections of the world of humanity. Therefore, endeavour as much as thou art able in order to illumine the lamp of thy heart by the light of love".* [1]

Bahá'u'lláh announced the Word of God to 'Abdu'l-Bahá, in Baghdád. Though still a young child, 'Abdu'l-Bahá recognized the Station of His Father and, throwing himself at the feet of Bahá'u'lláh, begged to be accepted as a sacrifice for His Cause. From that day, 'Abdu'l-Bahá gave His whole life to the service of Bahá'u'lláh and sacrificed every comfort in His path. 'Abdu'l-Bahá won the love and respect of Bahá'u'lláh's followers at a very early age, and later became known among them as "The Master". When Bahá'u'lláh passed away, His will, which is known as the *Book of the Covenant*, was opened. The Bahá'ís were happy to know that Bahá'u'lláh had appointed 'Abdu'l-Bahá as the Centre of His Covenant and as the authorized interpreter of His teachings.

The appointment of the Centre of the Covenant is a unique characteristic of the Bahá'í Faith. All the religions of the past became divided after the death of their Founders because the followers did not know where to turn after the Manifestation of God had left them. They started to interpret the teachings of God as they themselves understood them and, as they did not

---

[1] 'Abdu'l-Bahá: *Tablets of 'Abdu'l-Bahá*, Vol. III, pp. 674–75; and *The Divine Art of Living*, 2nd ed. 1986, pp. 29–30.

understand them the same way, these teachings were explained
in different forms. This became the cause of disunity among the
followers of the past religions. In the Bahá'í Faith, however, the
case has been different. Bahá'u'lláh, Who had come to remove
every form of disunity from the peoples of the world, did not
allow the Bahá'í Faith to become divided. He wrote a document
in which He appointed 'Abdu'l-Bahá as the one to whom all
Bahá'ís should turn for guidance in matters concerning His
teachings. This document, the *Book of the Covenant*, saved the
Bahá'ís from disunity. The *Book of the Covenant* preserved the
unity of the followers of Bahá'u'lláh but increased the jealousy
of 'Abdu'l-Bahá's half-brother, Muḥammad-'Alí. Like Yaḥyá
during the time of Bahá'u'lláh, Muḥammad-'Alí tried to bring
disunity among the Bahá'ís in the days of 'Abdu'l-Bahá. He
imagined that since he was a son of Bahá'u'lláh, he, too, could
make a claim to leadership. However, his efforts were useless
because his outward relationship with the Manifestation of God
was of no value when he did not obey what Bahá'u'lláh had
commanded. Muḥammad-'Alí was like a branch that had grown
out of a mighty Tree, but which could bear no fruit because it
had dried up and become worthless. And, like a withered
branch, he was cut off and thrown away.

When Muḥammad-'Alí failed to cause disunity among the
Bahá'ís, he joined hands with the enemies of the Cause and tried
to harm 'Abdu'l-Bahá. He poisoned the minds of government
officials against the Master and said that He was gathering
people around Him to rise up against the government. When
'Abdu'l-Bahá was building the Shrine of the Báb on Mount
Carmel, Muḥammad-'Alí reported that He was building a
fortress. This caused the Turkish Government send a special
party to the Holy Land to investigate the matter. Muḥammad-
'Alí succeeded in bribing the corrupt General, who came as the
head of the party, and false reports were sent to the Government
about 'Abdu'l-Bahá.

'Abdu'l-Bahá in the meantime, was giving every hour of His
life to the service of the Cause. The beautiful tablets that

streamed from His pen brought joy and inspiration to thousands of Bahá'ís in the world. Through His precious letters, He guided and strengthened their steps in the path of service to their Faith. When He was not occupied in writing, the Master was busy visiting the sick and seeing to the needs of the poor. From His scanty purse He freely gave to others, and no one ever turned away disappointed from the door of the Master's house.

'Abdu'l-Bahá paid little attention to the party of officials who had come to investigate the false charges brought against Him. Muḥammad-'Alí, on the other hand, showed them great respect and showered them with gifts and presents. Before they left, the General in charge of the party swore that he would come back to hang 'Abdu'l-Bahá at the city gate. This brought great rejoicing to the Master's enemies, while those who loved Him were filled with anxiety. Many of His friends begged 'Abdu'l-Bahá to flee from the Holy Land while there was still time, but the Master, whose trust was always in God, did not worry in the least. He said:

> *"To me prison is freedom, to me incarceration is an open court, to me humility is identical with glory, to me adversity is a gift and death is life."*[1]

The General who wanted to hang 'Abdu'l-Bahá, was himself killed in a war soon after he left the Holy Land. The Turkish Empire itself was broken up and a new regime took over the affairs of the government. Muḥammad-'Alí and the few others who had broken the Covenant of Bahá'u'lláh were frustrated in their efforts to harm 'Abdu'l-Bahá or to cause disunity among the Bahá'ís. They fell into disgrace and their shameful schemes became known to everyone.

'Abdu'l-Bahá's freedom came after nearly a lifetime of imprisonment when a new regime took over the government. At last the Master, who had served Bahá'u'lláh's Cause so faithfully under severe hardships, was free to move about and

---

[1]   'Abdu'l-Bahá: *Tablets of 'Abdu'l-Bahá*, Vol. III, p. 725.

take the Message of His Father to the people of other countries. The Bahá'ís of the West requested Him to travel to Europe and America and, though old in years and very weak from years of imprisonment, 'Abdu'l-Bahá graciously accepted their invitation.

'Abdu'l-Bahá spoke to thousands of people about the Bahá'í Faith during His journeys in the West. Sometimes he gave several lectures in one day. Both Bahá'ís and non-Bahá'ís came from far-off places to visit Him and hear His inspiring words. 'Abdu'l-Bahá was busy teaching the Cause wherever He went, from early morning until late at night. He did not think of Himself even when He was ill with fever and His friends begged Him to rest.

'Abdu'l-Bahá laid the cornerstone of the first Bahá'í House of Worship in the West—in the United States of America. It is now a beautiful building dedicated to the glory of the cause of God.

'Abdu'l-Bahá's travels in Europe and America produced wonderful results. The Bahá'í Faith was established in many countries, and before 'Abdu'l-Bahá passed away, He encouraged the believers to carry the new Message to other countries.

The Master passed away from this life in the Holy Land on the 28 November 1921. His resting place is in a room of the Shrine of the Báb next to that containing the remains of the Báb, a building that He Himself built during His lifetime.

'Abdu'l-Bahá was the Expounder of the Faith of God, the Interpreter of the Writings of Bahá'u'lláh, and the perfect Exemplar of His Teachings. Bahá'u'lláh called Him "*The Mystery of God*".[1]

---

1 Bahá'u'lláh quoted in: Shoghi Effendi, *God Passes By*, p. 242; and *World Order of Bahá'u'lláh*, pp. 134, 143–44.

Shoghi Effendi—The Guardian of the Faith

'Abdu'l-Bahá was like a loving father for the Bahá'ís. When He passed away the Bahá'ís of the world were very sad indeed. 'Abdu'l-Bahá's ministry had lasted about 30 years during which time the Bahá'ís had progressed under His unerring guidance and deepened their understanding in the teachings of Bahá'u'lláh. The Bahá'ís felt like orphans who had lost their wise and loving parent when 'Abdu'l-Bahá left this world. The enemies of the Cause on the other hand, and those who had broken the Covenant of Bahá'u'lláh, thought that this was the time for them to come forward and carry out their wicked plans. They thought that because 'Abdu'l-Bahá was not there to protect the unity of the Bahá'ís, it would be easy for them to attack the Cause. They did not know that God would not allow any breach in the unity of His Cause in this age.

'Abdu'l-Bahá had already provided for the unity of Bahá'u'lláh's followers. He, too, had made a firm covenant with Bahá'ís all over the world. He had left behind a wonderful Tablet—His *Will and Testament*—in which He had appointed His grandson, Shoghi Effendi, as the Guardian of the Faith of God.

The Bahá'ís lost a loving father with the passing of 'Abdu'l-Bahá, but in Shoghi Effendi they found a "true brother".

Shoghi Effendi was born in the blessed household of 'Abdu'l-Bahá. His mother was the daughter of 'Abdu'l-Bahá and His father was a close relative of the Báb. 'Abdu'l-Bahá has called him *"the most wondrous, unique and priceless pearl that doth gleam out from the twin surging seas"* and *"the sacred bough that hath branched out from the Twin Holy Trees"*[1] because in him the families of the Báb and Bahá'u'lláh were joined together. Shoghi Effendi grew up under the direct care and supervision of 'Abdu'l-Bahá. However, no one was aware of the station for which 'Abdu'l-Bahá was preparing him

---

[1] 'Abdu'l-Bahá: *Will and Testament*, p. 3.

although many saw signs of greatness in Shoghi Effendi long before 'Abdu'l-Bahá passed away. An American Bahá'í once wrote to the Master asking if she had correctly understood a prophecy mentioned in the Bible.[1] The prophecy indicated there should be a young child alive then who was destined to hold the helm of the Cause after 'Abdu'l-Bahá. The Master replied that she was right and that the blessed child was living and would soon illumine the world with his radiance.[2] To another person 'Abdu'l-Bahá gave the assurance that the blessed child would *"raise the Cause of God to great heights".*[3]

Shoghi Effendi was a young boy when the beloved Master wrote His *Will and Testament.* He was only twenty-four years of age when he became the Guardian of the Cause of God. It did not matter that he was not old in years because he was always assisted by Bahá'u'lláh. 'Abdu'l-Bahá called Shoghi Effendi the Sign of God on earth and said that all who obeyed him had obeyed God. It was through the great wisdom and spiritual guidance of Shoghi Effendi that the Message of Bahá'u'lláh was carried to every country of the globe.

Shoghi Effendi was studying in England at Oxford University when 'Abdu'l-Bahá passed away. His cherished desire was to serve the beloved Master throughout his life and to be able to translate the sacred Writings of the Bahá'í Faith into English for the thousands of believers who could not read them in Persian or Arabic. The news of the passing away of 'Abdu'l-Bahá was such a great blow to Shoghi Effendi that he became ill. Before he had fully recovered from the shock of being so suddenly separated from the Master, he arrived in the Holy Land to learn that 'Abdu'l-Bahá had given him the crushing responsibility of

---

1   Isaiah 11:6.
2   Amatu'l-Bahá Rúhíyyih Khánum Rabbani: *The Priceless Pearl*, p. 2; and the article "Twenty–five years of the Guardianship" in *The Bahá'í World*, Vol. XI, 1952, p. 114.
3   Amatu'l-Bahá Rúhíyyih Khánum Rabbani: "Twenty–five years of the Guardianship" in *The Bahá'í World*, Vol. XI, 1952, p. 114.

being the Guardian of the Cause of God. However, when God gives anyone a task to accomplish in this world, He also gives him the strength to undertake it. After many weeks spent in meditation and prayer, Shoghi Effendi was ready to start his great work in life. God blessed him with divine wisdom and inspiration in every step he took for the promotion of His Cause.

During the 36 years of his guardianship, Shoghi Effendi had no other thought but the progress of the Cause. He worked day and night, and did not spare himself in any way. His personal life was very simple. He seldom had more than one meal in twenty-four hours, nor slept more than a few hours every night. The rest of his time was given to his ever-growing work for the Cause of Bahá'u'lláh. Those who saw the quantity of work he accomplished, realized that it was only through the power of God that a simple man could do so much day after day and year after year.

The enemies of the Cause, who had hoped to carry out their evil designs after the passing of 'Abdu'l-Bahá, soon realized that the Faith of Bahá'u'lláh was now guarded by the iron arms of Shoghi Effendi. It was he who taught the Bahá'ís of the world how to work together to establish the World Order of Bahá'u'lláh, and how to carry out the instructions of 'Abdu'l-Bahá mentioned in His *Tablets of the Divine Plan*. In these Tablets, which the Master wrote to the Bahá'ís just before he passed away, He calls upon them all to arise for the promotion of the Cause, to forsake their homes and their comforts, and to carry the Message of Bahá'u'lláh to the far off corners of the world. Shoghi Effendi trained the Bahá'ís for years to prepare them for this great task. He taught them how to work through their local and national Assemblies, because unless the Bahá'ís learned to work as a united body, it would be impossible for them to accomplish anything. When they were prepared for the great undertaking, the Guardian encouraged them to scatter throughout the world and carry the banner of Bahá'u'lláh to every part of the globe. Under his divine guidance, hundreds of

Bahá'ís went out with the torch of Faith and settled in distant islands and territories to give the new Message to people everywhere.

The Bahá'í Faith had spread to 35 countries by the time of 'Abdu'l-Bahá's passing. During the lifetime of the beloved Guardian, the Message of Bahá'u'lláh was carried to over 251 countries of the world, including all the places mentioned by 'Abdu'l-Bahá in the *Tablets of the Divine Plan.*

In His *Will and Testament*, 'Abdu'l-Bahá called upon the Bahá'ís of the world to arise for the service of the Cause, and not to rest for a single moment until they had established the banner of the Faith in every part of the globe. Our dear Guardian carried out this request of the Master throughout his entire life and up to his very last day in this world. He passed away on the 4 November 1957, in London, where he had gone to buy materials for the construction of Bahá'í Institutions in the Holy Land.

The Guardian left us only after he was sure that his efforts during his 36 years of guardianship had given the universal Faith of Bahá'u'lláh a firm foundation. He knew that Bahá'u'lláh's work could then be continued by the Bahá'ís after he had gone. Like the perfect captain of a boat, he set the directions we were to follow and gave us the necessary instructions before he went away to rest. There could be no danger of our losing the way because the direction and the course we were to take were fixed by the Guardian himself. Under his spiritual guidance this Ark of God will surely reach its destination. During his lifetime, Shoghi Effendi drafted a Ten Year Plan that ended in 1963. This Plan required the Bahá'ís of the world to work closely together in taking the Message of Bahá'u'lláh to the remaining islands and territories of the globe where the Bahá'í Faith had not yet been established. The Guardian himself supervised the progress of this Plan in its early stages and, before he passed away, over 4,200 Bahá'í Centres had been established in the world, while Bahá'í literature had been translated into over 200 different languages,

In the Holy Land—the World Centre of the Faith—the Guardian built a beautiful superstructure over the Shrine of the Báb. He also built an International Archives building where the original Writings of the Báb and Bahá'u'lláh, as well as many other very precious relics are kept. These buildings and the lovely gardens surrounding them are one of the most beautiful spots in the world, and thousands of people come to visit them every year.

Shoghi Effendi completed his work by appointing 27 Hands of the Cause, whom he called the "Chief Stewards" of the Faith. He gave them the responsibility of protecting the Cause and of spreading the Teachings of Bahá'u'lláh. When the Guardian passed away, the Hands of the Cause elected a body of 9 from among themselves to remain in the Holy Land and see to the work at the World Centre. These were called the Custodians. The rest of the Hands scattered throughout the world to help in completing the Guardian's Ten Year Plan.

The end of the Ten Year Plan in 1963 marked a new milestone in the history of the Bahá'í Faith. A full century had passed since the day when Bahá'u'lláh had proclaimed His Mission. It was then that the Bahá'ís of the world elected the first Universal House of Justice—that Supreme Body that 'Abdu'l-Bahá has assured us will be under the direct guidance of God and infallible in all its decisions.

To celebrate this occasion, the Bahá'ís of the world were called to a great feast in London from 28 April to 2 May 1963. Over 6,200 people from all over the world attended this great festival. The unity of mankind was embodied in this grand celebration. Peoples of so many races and backgrounds, dressed in their national costumes, formed the beautiful garden of Bahá'u'lláh. That colourful audience in the Bahá'í World Congress was indeed the most befitting bouquet that we could offer to the precious memory of Shoghi Effendi, our beloved

Guardian, who had left us with the Ten Year Spiritual Crusade—a plan potent with so many victories and achievements.

Thanks to the untiring and ceaseless efforts of the beloved Guardian, the Bahá'ís of the world were well prepared for this tremendous new development in the progress of the Cause of God—the election of the Universal House of Justice. Shoghi Effendi, as 'Abdu'l-Bahá foretold, when he was still a child, did indeed raise the Cause of God to great heights!

Some of the
Teachings and Principles

Oneness of Mankind

Bahá'u'lláh has taught us the Oneness of Mankind. All human beings are the children of one God. If we believe in one Heavenly Father, then we must accept each other as brothers and sisters, as members of one family—the family of Man.

Before Bahá'u'lláh brought us the light of unity, there were many reasons that made men think they were different from others. Some people thought that because the colour of their skin was white, they were better than those who were black or yellow or brown. Bahá'u'lláh said this is not true. Man is not different because of his colour. If they are different, it is because they have received different degrees of education and not because they have different skin colours. The different coloured peoples of the world are like the different kinds of flowers you find in a garden. If all the flowers of a garden were of the same colour, it would not be so beautiful. Bahá'u'lláh said God is like a kind Shepherd for whom the white sheep are no better than the brown or the black. God loves us all, no matter what the colour of our skin may be or which part of the world we may come from. Why should we, then, look upon each other as strangers? Bahá'u'lláh has kindled such love in the hearts of His followers that they feel like members of the same family even though they come from all the countries of the world. In His Writings, Bahá'u'lláh says:

"O well-beloved ones! The tabernacle of unity hath been raised; regard ye not one another as strangers. Ye are the fruits

of one tree, and the leaves of one branch."[1]

"Be ye as the fingers of one hand, the members of one body. Thus counselleth you the Pen of Revelation ...."[2]

'Abdu'l-Bahá has written:

"And among the teachings of His Holiness Bahá'u'lláh is the oneness of the world of humanity; that all human beings are the sheep of God and He is the kind Shepherd. The Shepherd is kind to all the sheep, because He created them all, trained them, provided for them and protected them. There is no doubt that the Shepherd is kind to all the sheep and should there be among these sheep ignorant ones, they must be educated; if there be children, they must be trained until they reach maturity; if there be sick ones, they must be cured. There must be no hatred and enmity, for as by a kind physician these ignorant, sick ones should be treated."[3]

Let us pray for the unity of mankind:

"O my God! O my God! Unite the hearts of Thy servants, and reveal to them Thy great purpose. May they follow Thy commandments and abide in Thy law. Help them, O God, in their endeavour, and grant them strength to serve Thee. O God, leave them not to themselves, but guide their steps by the light of Thy knowledge, and cheer their hearts by their love. Verily, Thou art their Helper and their Lord."[4]

Removal of Prejudice

Bahá'u'lláh teaches that all forms of prejudice must be forgotten, whether it is national, racial or religious prejudice. As

---

[1] Bahá'u'lláh: *Tablets of Bahá'u'lláh*, p. 164; and *Gleanings from the Writings of Bahá'u'lláh*, Section CXII, p. 218.

[2] Bahá'u'lláh: *The Kitáb-i-Aqdas*, para. 58, p. 40; *Gleanings from the Writings of Bahá'u'lláh*, Section LXXI, p. 140; and *The Proclamation of Bahá'u'lláh*, p. 118.

[3] 'Abdu'l-Bahá: *Selections from the Writings of 'Abdu'l-Bahá*, pp. 298–99.

[4] Bahá'u'lláh: *Bahá'í Prayers* (US), p. 204.

long as people cling to prejudice, we will not have any peace on earth.

All the wars that we have had in the past, all the murders and the bloodshed have been due to prejudice of some kind. People have fought over their country or their religion, bringing destruction to the world and death to millions of their fellow humans.

'Abdu'l-Bahá says:

"If this prejudice and enmity are on account of religion consider that religion should be the cause of fellowship, otherwise it is fruitless. And if this prejudice be the prejudice of nationality consider that all mankind are of one nation; all have sprung from the tree of Adam, and Adam is the root of the tree. That tree is one and all these nations are like branches, while the individuals of humanity are like leaves, blossoms and fruits thereof. Then the establishment of various nations and the consequent shedding of blood and destruction of the edifice of humanity result from human ignorance and selfish motives.

"As to the patriotic prejudice, this is also due to absolute ignorance, for the surface of the earth is one native land. Everyone can live in any spot on the terrestrial globe. Therefore all the world is man's birth place. These boundaries and outlets have been devised by man. In the creation, such boundaries and outlets have been devised by man. In the creation, such boundaries and outlets were not assigned. Europe is one continent, Asia is one continent, Africa is one continent, Australia is one continent, but some of the souls, from personal motives and selfish interests, have divided each one of these continents and considered a certain part as their own country. God has set up no frontier between France and Germany; they are continuous. Yea, in the first centuries, selfish souls, for the promotion of their own interests, have assigned boundaries and outlets and have, day by day, attached more importance to these, until this led to intense enmity, bloodshed and rapacity in

subsequent centuries. In the same way this will continue indefinitely, and if this conception of patriotism remains limited within a certain circle, it will be the primary cause of the world's destruction. No wise and just person will acknowledge these imaginary distinctions. Every limited area which we call our native country we regard as our motherland, whereas the terrestrial globe is the motherland of all, and not any restricted area. In short, for a few days we live on this earth and eventually we are buried in it, it is our eternal tomb. Is it worth while that we should engage in bloodshed and tear one another to pieces for this eternal tomb? Nay, far from it, neither is God pleased with such conduct nor would any sane man approve of it.

"Consider! The blessed animals engaged in no patriotic quarrels. They are in the utmost fellowship with one another and live together in harmony. For example, if a dove from the east and a dove from the west, and a dove from the north and a dove from the south chance to arrive, at the same time, in one spot, they immediately associate in harmony. So is it with all the blessed animals and birds. But the ferocious animals, as soon as they meet, attack and fight with each other, tear each other to pieces and it is impossible for them to live peacefully together in one spot. They are all unsociable and fierce, savage and combative fighters."[1]

Search After Truth

When a child is born in a Christian family, he becomes a Christian. When the parents are Muslim, the children also become Muslims; if they are Hindus, their children become Hindus. Why? because most of the people of the world go on imitating their forefathers, and as long as this blind imitation is continued, people cannot become united. They fight over their imitations. Everyone claims that he has the truth and all the others are wrong. People seldom stop to think what would have happened if they had been born into another family with different beliefs. It is most likely that they would have beliefs

---

1   'Abdu'l-Bahá: *Selections from the Writings of 'Abdu'l-Bahá*, pp. 299–301.

quite different from those that they now believe to be the only true way.

Bahá'u'lláh teaches that Truth is one. If the people of the world would stop imitating their fathers and search after Truth for themselves, they would all reach the same conclusion and become united. The different peoples are like children who live in different houses and look at the sun through coloured window panes. However, as the colour of the panes in each house is different from that of the other houses, each child thinks the sun is a different colour. One child looks at the sun through green glass and thinks the colour of the sun is green. Another child looks through blue glass and thinks it is blue, and a third child believes the sun to be red because his window panes are red. These children may even quarrel over the colour of the sun, each believing what he sees to be the right colour. However, if they would stop looking at the sun through their little window panes, and step outside into the open, they would all see the true colour of the sun. Then there would be no further fights over the colour of the sun.

Bahá'u'lláh is calling upon the children of men to step out of the houses they have inherited from their great grand parents and stop looking at the sun through coloured window panes. For the sun we are looking at is the same sun, and once we remove the coloured glass from before our eyes, we will see it in its true colour.

God expects us to think about what we believe instead of following a certain belief for no better reason than that our forefathers have believed that way for many generations. If we all search after truth for ourselves, we will come to see that Truth is one; it can bring us together and make us forsake the differences of the past.

'Abdu'l-Bahá says:

"... the divine religions of the Holy Manifestations of God are in reality one, though in name and nomenclature they differ. Man must be a lover of the light, no matter from what dayspring it may appear. He must be a lover of the rose, no

matter in what soil it may be growing. He must be a seeker of the truth, no matter from what source it come. Attachment to the lantern is not loving the light. Attachment to the earth is not befitting, but enjoyment of the rose which develops from the soil is worthy. Devotion to the tree is profitless, but partaking of the fruit is beneficial. Luscious fruits, no matter upon what tree they grow or where they may be found, must be enjoyed. The word of truth, no matter which tongue utters it, must be sanctioned. Absolute verities, no matter in what book they be recorded, must be accepted. If we harbour prejudice, it will be the cause of deprivation and ignorance. The strife between religions, nations and races arises from misunderstanding. If we investigate the religions to discover the principles underlying their foundations, we will find they agree; for the fundamental reality of them is one and not multiple. By this means the religionists of the world will reach their point of unity and reconciliation. "[1]

At another place 'Abdu'l-Bahá says:

"Alas that humanity is completely submerged in imitations and unrealities, notwithstanding the truth of divine religion has ever remained the same. Superstitions have obscured the fundamental reality, the world is darkened, and the light of religion is not apparent. This darkness is conductive to differences and dissensions; rites and dogmas are many and various; therefore, discord has arisen among the religious systems, whereas religion is for the unification of mankind. True religion is the source of love and agreement amongst men, the cause of the development of praiseworthy qualities, but the people are holding to the counterfeit and imitation, negligent of the reality which unifies, so they are bereft and deprived of the radiance of religion. They follow superstitions inherited from their fathers and ancestors. To such an extent has this prevailed that they have taken away the heavenly light of divine truth and sit in the darkness of

---

1 'Abdu'l-Bahá: *The Promulgation of Universal Peace*, pp. 151–52.

imitations and imaginations. That which was meant to be conducive to life has become the cause of death; that which should have been an evidence of knowledge is now a proof of ignorance; that which was a factor in the sublimity of human nature has proved to be its degradation. Therefore, the realm of the reglionist has gradually narrowed and darkened, and the sphere of the materialist has widened and advanced; for the religionist has held to imitation and counterfeit, neglecting and discarding holiness and the sacred reality of religion. When the sun sets, it is the time for bats to fly. They come forth because they are creatures of the night. When the lights of religion become darkened, the materialists appear. They are the bats of night. The decline of religion is their time of activity; they seek the shadows when the world is darkened and clouds have spread over it."[1]

Bahá'u'lláh has risen from the eastern horizon. Like the glory of the sun He has come into the world. He has reflected the reality of divine religion, dispelled the darkness of imitations, laid the foundation of new teachings and resuscitated the world.

"The first teaching of Bahá'u'lláh is the investigation of reality. Man must seek reality himself, forsaking imitations and adherence to mere hereditary forms. As the nations of the world are following imitations in lieu of truth and as imitations are many and various, differences of belief have been productive of strife and warfare. So long as these imitations remain, the oneness of the world of humanity is impossible. Therefore, we must investigate reality in order that by its light the clouds and darkness may be dispelled. Reality is one reality; it does not admit multiplicity or division. If the nations of the world investigate reality, they will agree and become united. Many people and sects ... have sought reality through the guidance and teaching of Bahá'u'lláh. They have become united and now live in a

---

[1]   'Abdu'l-Bahá: *The Promulgation of Universal Peace*, pp. 179–80.

state of agreement and love; among them there is no longer the least trace of enmity and strife. ''[1]

Universal Language

One of the causes of misunderstanding in the world is that people cannot understand each other's language. Every country has a different tongue and when a person goes from his land to another part of the world, he feels that he is among strangers.

Bahá'u'lláh has come to unite all the peoples of the world and make them like members of the same family. One of His laws, therefore, is that a common language must be taught in every part of the world, so that every person will learn that language besides his own native tongue. In this way, people will feel at home, no matter where they go, because they can all understand each other.

The difference in language sometimes causes misunderstanding that may even lead to dangerous conflicts. Take the name of our Creator, for example. In the Hindi language He is called Ishwara, in Arabic Alláh and in English God. Ignorant people think that God is different from Ishwara or Alláh and fight with each other over these different names. When the people can all speak one common universal language, they will come to realize that they are all referring to the same Creator. This in itself will remove many misunderstandings among them.

The Bahá'ís have so far translated the Message of Bahá'u'lláh into over 800 languages of the world because people do not know one common language. When a universal language is adopted in the world, it will become much easier to give the teachings of Bahá'u'lláh to different peoples. Then everyone will be able to read the sacred Writings of the Manifestation of God Himself, in the universal language.

---

1   'Abdu'l-Bahá: *The Promulgation of Universal Peace*, p. 180.

Equality between Men and Women

A pigeon cannot fly if you cut off the feathers from one its wings, regardless of how strong its other wing may be, because a bird needs two wings to fly.

'Abdu'l-Bahá says:

"... the world of humanity possesses two wings: man and woman. If one wing remains incapable and defective, it will restrict the power of the other, and full flight will be impossible. Therefore, the completeness and perfection of the human world are dependent upon the equal development of these two wings."[1]

Again He says:

"God has created all creatures in couples. Man, beast, or vegetable, all the things of these three kingdoms are of two sexes, and there is absolute equality between them.

"In the vegetable world there are male plants and female plants; they have equal rights, and possess an equal share of the beauty of their species; though indeed the tree that bears fruit might be said to be superior to that which is unfruitful.

"In the animal kingdom we see that the male and the female have equal rights; and that they each share the advantages of their kind.

"Now in the two lower kingdoms of nature we have seen that there is no question of the superiority of one sex over the other. In the world of humanity we find a great difference; the female sex is treated as though inferior, and is not allowed equal rights and privileges. This condition is due not to nature, but to education. In the Divine Creation there is no such distinction. Neither sex is superior to the other in the sight of God."[2]

---

[1] 'Abdu'l-Bahá: *The Promulgation of Universal Peace*, p. 318.
[2] 'Abdu'l-Bahá: *Paris Talks*, pp. 160–61.

God has created us all as human beings, and it makes no difference to Him whether we are men or women. To a loving parent, sons and daughters are equally dear.

"Bahá'u'lláh has said that both [men and women] *belong to humankind and that in the estimation of God they are equal, for each is the complement of the other in the divine creative plan. The only distinction between them in the sight of God is the purity and righteousness of their deeds and actions, for that one is preferred by God who is most nearly in the spiritual image and likeness of the Creator."*[1]

Since God's bounty reaches man and woman alike, we should make no distinction between them. The duties of a man in a community may differ from those of a woman, but their rights and privileges must be equal. We should not think that a woman's talents are less than a man's. In the past women did not have the same education and opportunities as men, that is the reason they were not able to develop their different capacities.

When Bahá'ís are electing their Assemblies every year, the members they choose are those who are most sincere and capable. It does not make any difference whether they are men or women. We should always remember that God looks to the heart and character of a person and not the sex.

'Abdu'l-Bahá says:

"One whose thought is pure, whose education is superior, whose scientific attainments are greater, whose deeds of philanthropy excel, be that one man or woman, white or coloured, is entitled to full rights and recognition; there is no differentiation whatsoever."[2]

Universal Education

Another teaching of Bahá'u'lláh is that every child—boy or girl—must receive an education. If the parents neglect the

---

1   'Abdu'l-Bahá: *The Promulgation of Universal Peace*, p. 280.
2   'Abdu'l-Bahá: *The Promulgation of Universal Peace*, p. 166.

education of their children, they are responsible before God. This is the command of Bahá'u'lláh:

> *"Unto every father hath been enjoined the instruction of his son and daughter in the art of reading and writing ... He that putteth away that which is commanded unto him, the Trustees are then to take from him that which is required for their instruction if he be wealthy and, if not, the matter devolveth upon the House of Justice.   Verily have We made it [the House of Justice] a shelter for the poor and needy."*[1]

The education of children, therefore, is a compulsory and binding law for all Bahá'ís. If the parents can afford to educate their children but neglect to do so, then the Spiritual Assembly must force them to see to their education. However, if they are poor, the Spiritual Assembly must provide for the education of the children through the funds of the community.

Bahá'u'lláh states that the education of children is a sacred task. He says:

> *"He that bringeth up his son or the son of another, it is as though he hath brought up a son of Mine ...."*[2]

Is it not a privilege and a great honour for us to educate one of Bahá'u'lláh's children? We can receive this honour if only we educate our children or those of other people.

We cannot say that we need our young children to work at home, or take the cattle out to the pasture, so that they have no time to go to school. We must remember that looking after the cattle or working in the field is not a command of God, but education is.   If we do not obey this command, we are responsible. Similarly, we cannot say that our child is a girl and hence does not require any education. 'Abdu'l-Bahá said that there is equality between the rights of men and women. However, education is an example where, if a priority must be

---

[1]   Bahá'u'lláh: *The Kitáb-i-Aqdas*, para. 48, p. 37.
[2]   Bahá'u'lláh: *The Kitáb-i-Aqdas*, para. 48, p. 37.

given, it must be given to the girls. The reason for this is that the girls will become the mothers of the future, and an educated mother can bring up better children.

Education, according to Bahá'u'lláh, does not consist of only learning how to read and write. Children must also be educated in subjects that will enable them to serve the human race and virtues that will make them want to serve. At present children who live in different parts of the world are being brought up to be loyal to their country alone, and sometimes hatred towards another nation is engraved on their young minds. They are taught to be proud of being Germans, Arabs or Chinese and made to believe that their race, their religion or their special caste is the best in the world. According to Bahá'í Faith this is not correct. The aim of education must be to bring up men and women who believe that *"The earth is but one country, and mankind its citizens"*.[1] Then they will give their love and their services to the betterment of the whole world. If people adopt this method of education, it will take but one generation to establish the unity of all mankind.

Bahá'u'lláh also says:

"Schools must first train the children in the principles of religion, so that the Promise and the Threat recorded in the Books of God may prevent them from the things forbidden and adorn them with the mantle of the commandments; but this in such a measure that it may not injure the children by resulting in ignorant fanaticism and bigotry"[2]

This means that the spiritual values taught by the Manifestations of God must be the basis for every system of education. Only through spiritual enlightenment can man

---

1 Bahá'u'lláh: *Tablets of Bahá'u'lláh*, p. 167; *Gleanings from the Writings of Bahá'u'lláh*, Section CXVII, p. 250; and *The Proclamation of Bahá'u'lláh*, p. 116.
2 Bahá'u'lláh: *Tablets of Bahá'u'lláh*, p. 68.

become happier in life, because they will learn to live without any prejudice towards their fellowmen and be full of hope and confidence for the future. 'Abdu'l-Bahá writes:

> *"These schools ... must favour character and conduct above the sciences and arts. Good behaviour and high moral character must come first, for unless the character be trained, acquiring knowledge will only prove injurious. Knowledge is praiseworthy when it is coupled with ethical conduct and virtuous character; otherwise it is a deadly poison, a frightful danger. A physician of evil character, and who betrayeth his trust, can bring on death, and become the source of numerous infirmities and diseases."*[1]

Education must free us from superstitions and prejudices, and from the clutches of materialism. 'Abdu'l-Bahá writes:

> *'And among the teachings of Bahá'u'lláh is man's freedom, that through the ideal Power he should be free and emancipated from the captivity of the world of nature; for as long as man is captive to nature he is a ferocious animal, as the struggle for existence is one of the exigencies of the world of nature. This matter of the struggle for existence is the fountain-head of all calamities and is the supreme affliction."*[2]

A Bahá'í should never deprive his children from acquiring true knowledge, for according to Bahá'u'lláh:

> *"Knowledge is as wings to man's life, and a ladder for his ascent. Its acquisition is incumbent upon everyone. The knowledge of such sciences, however, should be acquired as can profit the peoples of the earth, and not those which begin with words and end with words. Great indeed is the claim of scientists and craftsmen on the peoples of the world. ...*

---

[1]   'Abdu'l-Bahá: *The Compilation of Compilations*, Vol. I (Education), p. 278.
[2]   'Abdu'l-Bahá: *Selections from the Writings of 'Abdu'l-Bahá*, p. 302

"In truth, knowledge is a veritable treasure for man, and a source of glory, of bounty, of joy, of exaltation, of cheer and gladness unto him."[1]

Religion and Science must Work Together

God has given us the power of thinking for ourselves so that we may be different from animals. Man has been able to progress down the ages, and to live very differently today than he used to thousands of years ago, because he can use his mind. New discoveries and inventions have made it possible for people to live in better homes and to fight against disease and ignorance. However, material progress is of little use to us if we do not also progress spiritually. God has given us religion to help us with our spiritual progress. Science without religion can do great harm but religion without science can also cause trouble. For the real progress of human race, both are necessary together. Science and religion must go hand and hand.

Science provides us with the tools and religion tells us how to use them. An axe or a sickle is a very useful thing if we use it correctly. However, if a murderer gets hold of an axe or a sickle, that useful tool becomes a dangerous weapon. The trouble with the world today is that science has provided people with useful tools that they can also use as weapons. The reason for this is that they have no religion to teach them how to make the best use of these tools. On the other hand, if we forsake science and stop using our mind and reason altogether, religion will become nothing but ignorance and superstition, and therefore harmful to the people of the world.

In the past people have thought that religion and science could not work together, but Bahá'u'lláh teaches that true religion agrees with true science. He tells us that our hearts and our minds can accept the same truths. 'Abdu'l-Bahá writes:

---

[1] Bahá'u'lláh: *Epistle to the Son of the Wolf*, pp. 26–27; and *Tablets of Bahá'u'lláh*, pp. 51–52.

"There is no contradiction between true religion and science. When a religion is opposed to science it becomes mere superstition: that which is contrary to knowledge is ignorance."[1]

We will conclude this chapter with a wonderful quotation from a talk by 'Abdu'l-Bahá:

"God made religion and science to be the measure ... of our understanding. Take heed that you neglect not such a wonderful power. Weigh all things in this balance.

"... Put all your beliefs into harmony with science; there can be no opposition, for truth is one. When religion, shorn of its superstitions, traditions and unintelligent dogmas, shows its conformity with science, then will there be a great unifying, cleansing force in the world which will sweep before it all wars, disagreements, discords and struggles—and then will mankind be united in the power of the Love of God."[2]

Extremes of Wealth and Poverty must End

Bahá'u'lláh tells us that He prefers justice to everything else in the world:

"O SON OF SPIRIT!

"The best beloved of all things in My sight is justice; turn not away therefrom if thou desirest Me ..."[3]

'Abdu'l-Bahá says:

"One of the most important principles of the Teaching of Bahá'u'lláh is:

"The right of every human being to the daily bread whereby they exist, or the equalization of the means of livelihood.

---

1   'Abdu'l-Bahá: Paris Talks, p. 141.
2   'Abdu'l-Bahá: Paris Talks, pp. 145–46.
3   Bahá'u'lláh: The Hidden Words of Bahá'u'lláh, (Arabic) No. 2.

"The arrangements of the circumstances of the people must be such that poverty shall disappear, that everyone, as far as possible, according to his rank and position, shall share in comfort and well-being.

"We see amongst us men who are overburdened with riches on the one hand, and on the other those unfortunate ones who starve with nothing; those who possess several stately palaces, and those who have not where to lay their head. Some we find with numerous courses of costly and dainty food; whilst others can scarcely find sufficient crusts to keep them alive. Whilst some are clothed in velvets, furs and fine linen, others have insufficient, poor and thin garments with which to protect them from the cold.

"This condition of affairs is wrong, and must be remedied."[1]

"Certainly, some being enormously rich and others lamentably poor, an organization is necessary to control and improve this state of affairs. It is [as] important to limit riches, as it is also of importance to limit poverty. Either extreme is not good. ...

"... When we see poverty allowed to reach a condition of starvation it is a sure sign that somewhere we shall find tyranny. Men must bestir themselves in this matter, and no longer delay in altering conditions which bring the misery of grinding poverty to a very large number of the people."[2]

There are a number of wonderful laws and teachings in the Bahá'í Faith for the creation of a balanced society where there are no extremes of wealth nor poverty. Many of these laws must be put into practice by the governments of the world, but the basic solution of the economic problems of today depends upon the individual. Bahá'ís are encouraged to make every effort towards material as well as spiritual advancement, but they should never forget these Words of Bahá'u'lláh:

---

1 'Abdu'l-Bahá: *Paris Talks*, p. 151.
2 'Abdu'l-Bahá: *Paris Talks*, p. 153.

"The essence of wealth is love for Me; whoso loveth Me is the possessor of all things, and he that loveth Me not is indeed of the poor and needy."[1]

True wealth for a Bahá'í then is the love of God in his heart. When he possesses this great treasure that no one can take away from him, then material riches will not be of great value in his eyes and outward poverty cannot be the cause of unhappiness.

Bahá'u'lláh says:

"O SON OF MY HANDMAID!

"Be not troubled in poverty nor confident in riches, for poverty is followed by riches, and riches are followed by poverty."[2]

Once our hearts are detached from the riches of this world, it becomes easy for us to share our wealth with those who are in need. This sharing is what Bahá'u'lláh expects His followers to do. In one of the Tablets of 'Abdu'l-Bahá we read:

"Among the teachings of Bahá'u'lláh is voluntary sharing of one's property with others among mankind. This voluntary sharing is greater than equality, and consists in this, that man should not prefer himself to others, but rather should sacrifice his life and property for others. But this should not be introduced by coercion so that it becomes a law and man is compelled to follow it. Nay, rather, should man voluntarily and of his own choice sacrifice his property and life for others, and spend willingly for the poor, just as is done in Persia among the Bahá'ís."[3]

No matter how poor a person may be, he can still find others who are poorer than himself and with whom he can share what he has. To the rich Bahá'u'lláh says:

"O YE RICH ONES ON EARTH!

---

[1] Bahá'u'lláh: *Tablets of Bahá'u'lláh*, p. 156.

[2] Bahá'u'lláh: *The Hidden Words of Bahá'u'lláh*, (Persian) No. 51.

[3] 'Abdu'l-Bahá: *Selections from the Writings of 'Abdu'l-Bahá*, p. 302.

"The poor in your midst are My trust; guard ye My trust, and be not intent only on your own case."[1]

He warns them not to forget those who are in need, for they will be punished if they are selfish:

"O CHILDREN OF DUST!
"Tell the rich of the midnight sighing of the poor, lest heedlessness may lead them into the path of destruction, and deprive them of the Tree of Wealth. To give and to be generous are attributes of Mine; well is it with him that adorneth himself with My virtues."[2]

Although the rich are called upon to give of their riches, Bahá'u'lláh forbids the poor to beg. He says that they must strive to earn their own living and place their trust in the Almighty. Every individual is called upon to *"... pursue his profession and calling in this world, to hold fast unto the Lord, to seek naught but His grace, inasmuch as in His hands is the destiny of all His servants."*[3]

We must never envy those who have more money than we do, for Bahá'u'lláh says:

"O SON OF EARTH!
"Know, verily, the heart wherein the least remnant of envy yet lingers, shall never attain My everlasting dominion, nor inhale the sweet savours of holiness breathing from My kingdom of sanctity."[4]

And again:

"O MY SERVANT!
"Purge thy heart from malice and, innocent of envy, enter the divine court of holiness."[5]

---

1   Bahá'u'lláh: *The Hidden Words of Bahá'u'lláh*, (Persian) No. 54.
2   Bahá'u'lláh: *The Hidden Words of Bahá'u'lláh*, (Persian) No. 49.
3   Bahá'u'lláh: *Tablets of Bahá'u'lláh*, p. 155.
4   Bahá'u'lláh: *The Hidden Words of Bahá'u'lláh*, (Persian) No. 6.
5   Bahá'u'lláh: *The Hidden Words of Bahá'u'lláh*, (Persian) No. 42.

We must know that wealth in itself is not a virtue. It can become a dangerous thing. Bahá'u'lláh says that God tests men with gold, just as gold is tested by fire. He also says.

"Know ye in truth that wealth is a mighty barrier between the seeker and his desire, the lover and his beloved. The rich, but for a few, shall in no wise attain the court of His presence nor enter the city of content and resignation. Well it is then with him, who, being rich, is not hindered by his riches from the eternal kingdom, nor deprived by them of imperishable dominion. By the Most Great Name! The splendour of such a wealthy man shall illuminate the dwellers of heaven even as the sun enlightens the people of the earth!"[1]

Our object in life, therefore, should not be the gathering of wealth to enjoy a short life of comfort in this world. Material riches can profit us only after we have acquired spiritual wealth and come to know ourselves and the purpose of our lives in this world.

Bahá'u'lláh has written:

"... man should know his own self and recognize that which leadeth unto loftiness or lowliness, glory or abasement, wealth or poverty. Having attained the stage of fulfilment and reached his maturity, man standeth in need of wealth, and such wealth as he acquireth through crafts or professions is commendable and praiseworthy in the estimation of men of wisdom, and especially in the eyes of servants who dedicate themselves to the education of the world and to the edification of its peoples."[2]

Whether we possess the riches of this world or not, let us remember that we can all be spiritually rich if we let the love of God enter into our hearts. This is what God tells every one of us through Bahá'u'lláh:

---

1   Bahá'u'lláh: *The Hidden Words of Bahá'u'lláh*, (Persian) No. 53.
2   Bahá'u'lláh: *Tablets of Bahá'u'lláh*, p. 35.

"O SON OF SPIRIT!

"I created thee rich, why dost thou bring thyself down to poverty? Noble I made thee, wherewith dost thou abase thyself? Out of the essence of knowledge I gave thee being, why seekest thou enlightenment from anyone beside Me? Out of the clay of love I moulded thee, how dost thou busy thyself with another? Turn thy sight unto thyself, that thou mayest find Me standing within thee, mighty, powerful and self-subsisting."[1]

Happiness

One of Bahá'u'lláh's great bounties to us is the joy and happiness He has created in our hearts. We are joyful because the love of God is within us. We are happy because we know the meaning and purpose of our short lives on this earth. We rejoice because we have found our Beloved, and through the influence of His creative Words are now at peace with the rest of humanity

Bahá'u'lláh says:

"O My friends that dwell upon the dust! Haste forth unto your celestial habitation. Announce unto yourselves the joyful tidings: 'He Who is the Best-Beloved is come! He hath crowned Himself with the glory of God's Revelation, and hath unlocked to the face of men the doors of His ancient Paradise.' Let all eyes rejoice, and let every ear be gladdened, for now is the time to gaze on His beauty, now is the fit time to hearken to His voice. Proclaim unto every longing lover: 'Behold, your Well-Beloved hath come among men!' and to the messengers of the Monarch of love impart the tidings: 'Lo, the Adored One hath appeared arrayed in the fullness of His glory!' O lovers of His beauty! Turn the anguish of your separation from Him into the joy of an everlasting reunion ...."[2]

---

[1] Bahá'u'lláh: *The Hidden Words of Bahá'u'lláh*, (Arabic) No. 13.

[2] Bahá'u'lláh: *Gleanings from the Writings of Bahá'u'lláh*, Section CLI, p. 320.

The joy of having recognized the Beloved and of hearkening to His voice fills the heart of every Bahá'í. This great bounty was felt by the thousands of Bahá'í martyrs who were glad to give their precious lives for the sake of their Beloved. When the joy of Faith takes possession of our heart, nothing on this earth can discourage us or make us unhappy. Poverty, sickness and hardship can be forgotten when the love of God and His creatures is in our hearts.

'Abdu'l-Bahá often mentioned the continuous happiness that He felt even when He was living in prison under very severe conditions. He wrote:

> *"... I was happy in imprisonment. I was in the utmost elation because I was not a criminal. They had imprisoned me in the path of God. ... I was happy that—praise be to God!—I was a prisoner in the Cause of God, that my life was not wasted, that it was spent in the Divine service. Nobody who saw me imagined that I was in prison. They beheld me in the utmost joy, complete thankfulness and health, paying no attention to the prison."*[1]

The happiness that comes through the love we feel for God and our fellow creatures makes us more worthy of giving praise to the Almighty and of receiving His blessings. Bahá'u'lláh has written:

> *"O SON OF MAN!*
> *"Rejoice in the gladness of thine heart, that thou mayest be worthy to meet Me and to mirror forth My beauty"*[2]

Bahá'ís should always reflect the radiant light of happiness. How can we be unhappy when we read these wonderful Words of Bahá'u'lláh?:

> *"O SON OF SPIRIT!*

---

[1] 'Abdu'l-Bahá: *The Promulgation of Universal Peace*, p. 225.
[2] Bahá'u'lláh: *The Hidden Words of Bahá'u'lláh*, (Arabic) No. 36.

"With the joyful tidings of light I hail thee: rejoice! To the court of holiness I summon thee; abide therein that thou mayest live in peace for evermore."[1]

Bahá'u'lláh says that the heart is the seat of God. When the heart has known the joy of receiving its Beloved, no happiness on earth can compare with it. The wealth of the world cannot add to this happiness, nor can the lack of prosperity become a cause of sorrow to such a heart.

The joy that comes with the pleasures of this world is not true happiness because it does not endure. Bahá'u'lláh tells us not to be affected by it:

"O SON OF MAN!
"Should prosperity befall thee, rejoice not, and should abasement come upon thee, grieve not, for both shall pass away and be no more."[2]

'Abdu'l-Bahá says:

"When a man is thirsty he drinks water. When he is hungry he eats food. But if a man be not thirsty, water gives him no pleasure and if his hunger be already satisfied, food is distasteful to him.

"This is not so with spiritual enjoyments. Spiritual enjoyments bring always joy. The love of God brings endless happiness. These are joys in themselves and not alleviations.
...

"God created in us a divine holy spirit—the human spirit with its intellectual powers which are above the powers of nature. By this we enjoy the ecstasies of the spirit and see the world illumined. ... This power distinguishes you above all other creatures, why do you devote it only to your material conditions? This is that which should be used for

---

1   Bahá'u'lláh: *The Hidden Words of Bahá'u'lláh*, (Arabic) No. 33.
2   Bahá'u'lláh: *The Hidden Words of Bahá'u'lláh*, (Arabic) No. 52.

*the acquisition and manifestation of the bounties of God, that
ye may establish the Kingdom of God among men and attain
to happiness in both worlds, the visible and the invisible.*"[1]

Let us be happy because we are living in such a wonderful
age. Let us enjoy the paradise that God has prepared for us
where men live as brothers, and where the strifes and differences
of the past are forgotten.

Let us rejoice in these words of 'Abdu'l-Bahá:

> "*GOOD NEWS! GOOD NEWS!*
> *For Everlasting Life is here!*
> *O Ye that sleep, Awake!*
> *O ye heedless ones, Learn wisdom!*
> *O Blind, receive your sight!*
> *O Deaf, Hear!*
> *O Dumb, Speak!*
> *O Dead, Arise!*
> *Be Happy!*
> *Be Happy!*
> *Be full of joy.*"[2]

Immortality

Our lives are very short. Twenty or thirty years may seem a long
time when we are still very young, but when we have left those
years behind us, we wonder how they could have gone by so
swiftly. The years that lie ahead of us will also pass like fleeting
moments, and death will soon overtake us all.

Is death the end of everything for us? No! The Bahá'í Faith
teaches that death is not the end. It is only a beginning.

Bahá'u'lláh says:

> "*O SON OF THE SUPREME!*

---

1 'Abdu'l-Bahá: *The Divine Art of Living*, 1974 ed., pp. 16–17.
2 'Abdu'l-Bahá: *'Abdu'l-Bahá in London*, Notes of Conversations, pp. 126–27.

"I have made death a messenger of joy to thee. Wherefore dost thou grieve? I made the light to shed on thee its splendour. Why dost thou veil thyself therefrom?"[1]

Death is the beginning of our spiritual journey towards God. It is a rebirth—a spiritual rebirth.

When our soul departs from our body, it continues to live and to progress in the Kingdom of God. But it never comes back to the earth in a material form.

A nightingale that has always lived in a cage does not know any other place but the cage. It may get glimpses of a garden through the bars of its cage. However, the poor bird has no idea of freedom and has never known the joy of flying in the green woods or the open fields. If you open the door of the cage to set the bird free, it may hop to a corner of the cage but not want to leave it. When you put your hand in to take the bird out, it will become frightened and will try to escape from your hand. However, once the bird is free it will soar high in the open sky, and sing among the green trees. It makes its home in the flowered meadows and the perfumed woods, and never comes back to a cage even if you offer it thousands of golden cages.

Similarly, when the soul is set free from the cage of this body, those who are not aware of the Kingdom of God and the happiness that awaits them after they depart from this life, will find it very difficult to let go of this life. It is because they know only of the cage, and are unaware of the heaven of God's love and eternal mercy

Those who have recognized the Manifestations of God, however, are sure of the immortality of the soul and everlasting life. Somebody asked Bahá'u'lláh about life after death, and this was His reply:

"And now concerning thy question regarding the soul of man and its survival after death. Know thou of a truth that the

---

1   Bahá'u'lláh: *The Hidden Words of Bahá'u'lláh,* (Arabic) No. 32.

soul, after its separation from the body, will continue to progress until it attaineth the presence of God, in a state and condition which neither the revolution of ages and centuries, nor the changes and chances of this world, can alter. It will endure as long as the Kingdom of God, His sovereignty, His dominion and power will endure. It will manifest the signs of God and His attributes, and will reveal His loving-kindness and bounty. The movements of My pen is stilled when it attempteth to befittingly describe the loftiness and glory of so exalted a station."[1]

Death is spiritual rebirth for each one of us. Let us therefore be prepared to welcome *"the messenger of joy"*[2] whenever it may knock at our door.

Heaven and Hell

You will be rewarded with a rich harvest if you plant a field in the proper season, water it regularly and protect it from pests and birds. However, if you do not sow your seeds at the right time, and neglect to water the field, you cannot hope for a good crop. You will be punishable for your negligence when the time comes to reap the harvest and who can be blamed for the loss except yourself?

Reward and punishment are necessary for order to exist in the world. Reward and punishment are the natural consequences of our deeds. All the Messengers of the past have tried to make us realize that what we do in this world not only affects our lives here, but continues to bear results after our death. If our deeds are good, they will produce good results and become the cause of everlasting happiness; if they are bad, they will bear evil results and bring eternal suffering to us. God does not wish to take revenge on those who have done wrong. However, it is impossible to get good results from bad actions, just as it is

---

1 Bahá'u'lláh: *Gleanings from the Writings of Bahá'u'lláh*, Section LXXXI, pp. 155–56.

2 Bahá'u'lláh: *The Hidden Words of Bahá'u'lláh*, (Arabic) No. 32.

impossible to have beautiful flowers in the garden when we have planted weeds. This is what is meant by reward and punishment. However, this essential belief, which has been taught in all religions, has been greatly misunderstood.

The manifestations of God have explained the existence of reward and punishment through symbols and parables. We have mentioned that the Manifestations of God are perfect Educators. A perfect educator must necessarily teach in a way that his students may understand or else there would be no purpose in His teaching. God's Messengers have pictured a life full of joy and pleasure for the good, and spoken of torture and misery for the wicked. They have done this to help people understand that they will have to account for their deeds after their life in this world has ended. The pleasures and tortures they have mentioned are those that people know of in this world because it was the only way to make people understand the importance of Their teachings on life after death.

To a small child who asks about knowledge, the parent may say that it is sweeter than anything he has ever enjoyed. Of course, the parent does not mean that knowledge is a type of food that can be tasted. When the child is older, he will come to know what his parent meant by the description he gave. Most of the people in the world are taking the symbols and parables that the Manifestations of God have used about life after death quite literally. The people do not realize that they were meant to illustrate spiritual experiences. They have, therefore, set up an imaginary hell and heaven. Some believe hell to be a horrible place with fire, disease and horrid devils in which sinners are tortured forever. Heaven, according to them, is a beautiful garden full of delicious fruits and earthly pleasures. Others believe that our souls will return to this world after death as if there were no other place in the whole of the universe except our little planet. They say that we will come back in different forms, and that we may even come as animals depending on the kind of deeds that we have done in our lifetime.

Whereas the Manifestations of the past have had to speak of our experiences after death in symbolic terms, Bahá'u'lláh says we are now ready to know the true meaning of heaven and hell. The two important facts that we must remember are these:

1. Our souls are immortal and continue to live after our bodies die.
2. Our deeds in this world will produce their results even after the soul departs from the body.

The world into which the soul enters after departing from the body is very different from the world that we are used to here. 'Abdu'l-Bahá says it is as different from this world as our world is different from the womb of the mother where a child lives before it is born. A child prepares for his life in this world by developing his eyes, ears and limbs that he does not need in his mother's womb. However, he cannot live a normal, healthy life here without these physical features. Similarly, we too must prepare for a happy life in the next world that our souls will be born into after leaving this world. In the next world, we are not going to need physical eyes and ears any more. There we will need spiritual qualities that we can acquire in this world by following the teachings of God sent to us through His Messengers.

There is, however, a great difference between the condition of a child in his mother's womb and that of a person who is living in this world. The unborn child is not responsible for his development because he is helpless. However, in this world we are given the power to choose between right and wrong, good and bad. We are, therefore, responsible for our spiritual development. If we fail to grow strong and healthy in spirit, then we are going to be very unhappy in the next world. This state of unhappiness is called hell. If on the other hand, we strive to understand and obey the laws of God, we will be preparing for a life of happiness in the next world and we will enjoy the state that is spoken of as heaven. Bahá'u'lláh says that heaven is nearness to God and hell is being deprived of this bounty. He calls upon each one of us to strive to become worthy of the eternal blessings that are prepared for us in the worlds to come:

> *"O SON OF BOUNTY!*
>
> *"Out of the wastes of nothingness, with the clay of My command I made thee to appear, and have ordained for thy training every atom in existence and the essence of all created things. Thus, ere thou didst issue from thy mother's womb, I destined for thee two founts of gleaming milk, eyes to watch over thee, and hearts to love thee. Out of My loving-kindness, 'neath the shade of My mercy I nurtured thee, and guarded thee by the essence of My grace and favour. And My purpose in all this was that thou mightest attain My everlasting dominion and become worthy of My invisible bestowals. ..."*[1]

Miracles

The Manifestations of God are endowed with great powers. They are able to perform things that are impossible for other people to do. Their great miracles are: Their teachings, Their personal lives, and the influence of Their words on the hearts of men for centuries after They Themselves have left this world. These miracles have been performed by all the Manifestations of God.

The Messengers of God use no worldly means or power to influence people, yet They have always been opposed by the forces of the state and all the powerful, learned people of Their time. Those who first believed in Them have usually been poor and insignificant people, without any worldly position. In spite of all this, Their Message has spread to conquer the world and create new civilizations. This story has been repeated in every age, and with the coming of every Manifestation a new civilization has been established in the world. When we hear of the civilizations that the Hindus, Jews, Christians or Moslems

---

1   Bahá'u'lláh: *The Hidden Words of Bahá'u'lláh*, (Persian) No. 29.

developed during past ages, we must remember that the Founder of each of these great movements was but a single Messenger of God. Each Messenger, in His days, initially stood alone against the forces of the whole world, and still They were victorious! What greater miracle do we need to prove the truth of these Manifestations of God!

There are many people who believe that the proof of prophethood lies in the performance of some difficult task that is usually expected of a magician. The followers of each religion relate extraordinary things about the Founder of their Faith to prove that He was a true Manifestation of God. The Hindus say that one day the feet of baby Krishna touched the river Yamuna while He was being carried by His father. The water immediately receded to allow Him to be carried to the other side. The Christians say that Jesus Christ satisfied the hunger of hundreds of people with a few loaves of bread. Similar miracles are attributed to Zoroaster, Buddha, Moses and Muḥammad by Their followers.

Bahá'ís believe that all the Manifestations of God have been capable of accomplishing extraordinary things. However, such deeds are neither convincing to those who do not believe in Them, nor can they be used as proofs of Their Prophethood. A Christian, for instance, may tell a Jew or a Buddhist that Jesus Christ gave life to a dead person. However, his words will have little effect on the person who does not believe in Jesus. It certainly will not convince him that Jesus Christ was a Manifestation of God. He may even say that it is only the followers of Jesus Christ who have attributed this miracle to Him. Even those who lived in the days of Jesus did not believe in Him because of His miracles. However, if the Christian points out how the beautiful teachings of Jesus Christ have brought eternal life to millions of people who were spiritually dead, or refers to the saintly life of Jesus Christ Himself that has inspired the hearts of many generations of the human race, no one can deny it. The life of Jesus Christ and His teachings are by far greater miracles than His having raised to life one or two people who might have lived for a few more years and died again.

The Manifestations of God are divine Physicians. What we should expect from them is a prescription that will cure our spiritual ailments. It is foolish of us to expect them to prove their Prophethood through the demonstration of magical performances. We do not ask a doctor who has come to prescribe for a patient to prove his skill by jumping from the roof. The only way the doctor can prove that he is indeed what he claims to be, is to cure his patient. That is why Bahá'u'lláh, despite those who were with Him seeing Him accomplish extraordinary things, has forbidden Bahá'ís to mention them as proofs of His greatness. The following incident, which occurred when Bahá'u'lláh was in Baghdád, shows how valueless these so-called miracles can be.

A council of Muslim divines, who knew that they could not deny the Truth of Bahá'u'lláh through argument and logic, asked Him to perform a miracle for them. They hoped that Bahá'u'lláh would refuse and thus give them an excuse to denounce Him. They chose one of the greatest Mullás from among themselves to deliver the message to Bahá'u'lláh. His reply to them was that the Cause of God was not a plaything and that He had not come to set up a magical show to please the whims and fancies of the people. However, if they could all decide upon a particular feat, no matter how impossible it might seem, then Bahá'u'lláh would accomplish it before their eyes. The only condition was that when the miracle was performed, they would all accept Him as the Promised One.

The Mullás did not accept the condition. They were afraid that Bahá'u'lláh might perform the miracle and then they would have no excuse for denying His claim. So they dispersed without asking Bahá'u'lláh for any miracle.

This incident clearly shows that miracles, even if performed, do not serve to prove anything to those who have already decided to deny the Truth. For those who are just in their judgement and willing to understand, the teachings of the Manifestations of God are in themselves true and lasting miracles.

Moral and Ethical Teachings

One of the principles of the Bahá'í Faith is that the foundation of all religions is one. The moral principles of all religions are certainly a part of the foundation of the religions. Therefore, they are similar.

In the teachings of Bahá'u'lláh, we find very high standards of ethics and personal conduct. We can say that almost all the teachings of Bahá'u'lláh influence the personal conduct and behaviour of man. In the Revelation of Bahá'u'lláh, there are literally thousands of Tablets revealed by the Báb, Bahá'u'lláh and 'Abdu'l-Bahá, and in the writings of Shoghi Effendi setting the pattern of Bahá'í life based on purity of mind and action. We are not able to compile all these beautiful writings into one large book. Nevertheless it is appropriate to have some glimpses of these beautiful writings from the Bahá'í Scriptures.

Readers of this book will have to continue their studies to immerse themselves in the immeasurable ocean of the Holy Writings if they wish to bring out such treasures and incomparable gems.

Bahá'u'lláh writes to one of His sons:

"Be generous in prosperity, and thankful in adversity. Be worthy of the trust of thy neighbour, and look upon him with a bright and friendly face. Be a treasure to the poor, an admonisher to the rich, an answerer of the cry of the needy, a preserver of the sanctity of thy pledge. Be fair in thy judgement, and guarded in thy speech. Be unjust to no man, and show all meekness to all men. Be as a lamp unto them that walk in darkness, a joy to the sorrowful, a sea for the thirsty, a haven for the distressed, an upholder and defender of the victim of oppression. Let integrity and uprightness distinguish all thine acts. Be a home for the stranger, a balm

to the suffering, a tower of strength for the fugitive. Be eyes to the blind, and a guiding light unto the feet of the erring. Be an ornament to the countenance of truth, a crown to the brow of fidelity, a pillar of the temple of righteousness, a breath of life to the body of mankind, an ensign of the hosts of justice, a luminary above the horizon of virtue, a dew to the soil of the human heart, an ark on the ocean of knowledge, a sun in the heaven of bounty, a gem on the diadem of wisdom, a shining light in the firmament of thy generation, a fruit upon the tree of humility."[1]

Here are more quotations from the Holy Writings pertaining to personal conduct:

"All men have been created to carry forward an ever-advancing civilization. ... To act like the beasts of the field is unworthy of man. Those virtues that befit his dignity are forbearance, mercy, compassion and loving-kindness towards all the peoples and kindreds of the earth."[2]

"To transgress the limits of one's own rank and station is, in no wise, permissible. The integrity of every rank and station must needs be preserved. By this is meant that every created thing should be viewed in the light of the station it hath been ordained to occupy."[3]

*   *   *

"Charity is pleasing and praiseworthy in the sight of God and is regarded as a prince among goodly deeds. ... Blessed is he who preferreth his brother before himself. Verily, such a man is reckoned, by virtue of the Will of God, ... with the people of Bahá ...."[4]

---

1   Bahá'u'lláh: *Epistle to the Son of the Wolf*, pp. 93–4; and *Gleanings from the Writings of Bahá'u'lláh*, Section CXXX, p. 285.

2   Bahá'u'lláh: *Gleanings from the Writings of Bahá'u'lláh*, Section CIX, p. 215.

3   Bahá'u'lláh: *Gleanings from the Writings of Bahá'u'lláh*, Section XCIII, p. 188.

4   Bahá'u'lláh: *Tablets of Bahá'u'lláh*, p. 71.

"They who are possessed of riches, however, must have the utmost regard for the poor, for great is the honour destined by God for those poor who are steadfast in patience. ... There is no honour, except what God may please to bestow, that can compare to this honour. Great is the blessedness awaiting the poor that endure patiently and conceal their sufferings, and well is it with the rich who bestow their riches on the needy and prefer them before themselves."[1]

*　　　　　*　　　　　*

"To look after the sick is one of the greatest duties. For every soul who becomes sick, the other friends should certainly offer their lives (in service) with the utmost kindness."[2]

*　　　　　*　　　　　*

"We, verily, have chosen courtesy, and made it the true mark of such as are nigh unto Him. Courtesy is, in truth, a raiment which fitteth all men, whether young or old. Well is it with him that adorneth his temple therewith, and woe unto him who is deprived of this great bounty."[3]

"O people of God! I admonish you to observe courtesy, for above all else it is the prince of virtues. Well is it with him who is illumined with the light of courtesy and is attired with the vesture of uprightness. Whoso is endued with courtesy hath indeed attained a sublime station."[4]

*　　　　　*　　　　　*

"Beware lest ye prefer yourselves above your neighbours."[5]

---

[1] Bahá'u'lláh: *Gleanings from the Writings of Bahá'u'lláh*, Section C, p. 202.

[2] 'Abdu'l-Bahá: *Tablets of 'Abdu'l-Bahá*, Vol. I, p. 149; and *Lights of Guidance*, No. 946, p. 282.

[3] Bahá'u'lláh: *Epistle to the Son of the Wolf*, p. 50; and *The Proclamation of Bahá'u'lláh*, p. 20.

[4] Bahá'u'lláh: *Tablets of Bahá'u'lláh*, p. 88.

[5] Bahá'u'lláh: *Gleanings from the Writings of Bahá'u'lláh*, Section CXVI, p. 315.

"Be fair to yourselves and to others, that the evidences of justice may be revealed, through your deeds, among Our faithful servants."[1]

"... equity is the most fundamental among human virtues. The evaluation of all things must needs depend upon it."[2]

"Say: Observe equity in your judgement, ye men of understanding heart! He that is unjust in his judgement is destitute of the characteristics that distinguish man's station."[3]

* * *

"We love to see you at all times consorting in amity and concord within the paradise of My good-pleasure, and to inhale from your acts the fragrance of friendliness and unity, of loving-kindness and fellowship. ... We shall always be with you; if We inhale the perfume of your fellowship, Our heart will assuredly rejoice, for naught else can satisfy Us."[4]

* * *

"The poor in your midst are My trust; guard ye My trust, and be not intent only on your own ease."[5]

"If ye encounter one who is poor, treat him not disdainfully. Reflect upon that whereof ye were created. Every one of you was created of sorry germ."[6]

* * *

"A kindly tongue is the lodestone of the hearts of men. It is the bread of the spirit, it clotheth the words with meaning, it is the fountain of the light of wisdom and understanding."[1]

---

1 Bahá'u'lláh: *Gleanings from the Writings of Bahá'u'lláh*, Section CXXVIII, p. 278.
2 Bahá'u'lláh: *Gleanings from the Writings of Bahá'u'lláh*, Section C, p. 203.
3 Bahá'u'lláh: *Gleanings from the Writings of Bahá'u'lláh*, Section C, p. 204.
4 Bahá'u'lláh: *Gleanings from the Writings of Bahá'u'lláh*, Section CXLVI, pp. 315–16.
5 Bahá'u'lláh: *The Hidden Words*, (Persian) No. 54.
6 Bahá'u'lláh: *Epistle to the Son of the Wolf*, p. 55.

"Each sees in the other the Beauty of God reflected in the soul, and finding this point of similarity, they are attracted to one another in love. This love will make all men the waves of one sea, this love will make them all the stars of one heaven and the fruits of one tree. This love will bring the realization of true accord, the foundation of real unity."[2]

"Love is unlimited, boundless, infinite! Material things are limited, circumscribed, finite."[3]

"It is clear that limited material ties are insufficient to adequately express the universal love.

"The great unselfish love for humanity is bounded by none of these imperfect, semi-selfish bounds; this is the one perfect love, possible to all mankind, and can only be achieved by the power of the Divine Spirit."[4]

*   *   *

"Deal not treacherously with the substance of your neighbour. Be ye trustworthy on earth, and withhold not from the poor the things given unto you by God through His grace. He, verily, will bestow upon you the double of what ye possess."[5]

*   *   *

"Fair speech and truthfulness, by reason of their lofty rank and position, are regarded as a sun shining above the horizon of knowledge."[6]

---

[1] Bahá'u'lláh: *Epistle to the Son of the Wolf*, p. 15: and *Gleanings from the Writings of Bahá'u'lláh*, Section CXXXII, p. 289.

[2] 'Abdu'l-Bahá: *Paris Talks*, pp. 100–01.

[3] 'Abdu'l-Bahá: *Paris Talks*, p. 36.

[4] 'Abdu'l-Bahá: *Paris Talks*, p. 37.

[5] Bahá'u'lláh: *Epistle to the Son of the Wolf*, pp. 54–55.

[6] Bahá'u'lláh: *Tablets of Bahá'u'lláh*, p. 40.

Administration

Religion without Priests

There was a time when it was necessary to have a group of people in society to be in charge of religious affairs. Ordinary people were either illiterate or did not have time to make a proper study of their religion. They therefore engaged a number of people who had no other task or profession in life than to study religion and to see that people observed its laws. That is why we find Brahmins among the Hindus, Bhikkhus among the Buddhists, priests among the Christians and Mullás among the Muslims.

In the Bahá'í Faith, one of its distinctions is that a professional priesthood is abolished. Bahá'u'lláh says that although it was necessary to have priests in the past, they are not needed in our age. He has called upon every one of us to search after Truth for himself. Hence, we may see with our own eyes and not with the eyes of others, hear with our own ears, and understand with our own power of reason. Bahá'ís are expected to acquire more knowledge about their Faith by searching after Truth for themselves. This may not be the case with people of other religions who expect to receive their instruction from clergymen. Every Bahá'í has to pray for himself. He cannot pay another man to pray for him as is done by many people in other religions. A Bahá'í asks for God's grace and forgiveness himself and does not need a priest to do it for him through man-made rituals and ceremonies. Every Bahá'í can establish contact with God through His Manifestation, and no medium is required between him and Bahá'u'lláh.

Although there have been many good priests in every religion, much of the harm done in the name of religion has been due to the priests in every age. There were two priests living in one neighbourhood that did not always agree on religious problems, and their disagreement brought a great deal of trouble to the world. Some people thought one priest was right, while other people believed that the other priest's views were correct. In this manner, disunity and divisions have arisen in every religion. Gradually many sects were formed as men quarrelled with each other over different interpretations of their sacred writings, and eventually this became the cause of wars and bloodshed.

Such conflicts cannot occur in the Bahá'í Faith. Firstly, there are no priests or other personalities in the Faith who can form a following among the believers. All are equal in the Faith. Secondly, nobody has the right to interpret the teachings and Writings of Bahá'u'lláh. This authority was given only to 'Abdu'l-Bahá by Bahá'u'lláh Himself, and after 'Abdu'l-Bahá the right of interpretation was given to Shoghi Effendi alone.

It is dangerous that a living can be earned through religion. The danger arises because many insincere people may be attracted to this profession for no other reason than that they want to live an easy life or have a good income. Such people have always misled others in the garb of the priesthood, and have committed many crimes in the name of religion to serve their own selfish interests.

Bahá'u'lláh has abolished the institution of the priesthood so that no one can ever hope to misuse religion to serve his own selfish and worldly desires.

The history of the past shows that whenever a Manifestation of God appeared in the world, priests of the previous religions were the first to oppose Him. Why? because those priests knew that by believing in the new Manifestation, they would have to sacrifice their positions, their wealth and material comforts. They therefore did their best to uproot the new religion when it appeared among them. Buddhism was pushed out of India by the priests of the time. Jesus Christ was crucified because the

Jewish priests opposed Him. The Báb was martyred because Muslim priests did not want people to follow Him. Bahá'u'lláh suffered all His life chiefly because the Mullás instigated the government and the people of their time to rise against the new Cause of God.

There were exceptions of course. Many learned priests who lived at the time of the Báb and Bahá'u'lláh believed in Them, and some even shed their blood in the path of God. However, when they accepted the Báb and Bahá'u'lláh, they became Bahá'ís—humble servants of the Cause of God—they were no longer priests. They took up other professions with which to earn their livelihood. They did not mingle money with religion or a worldly profession with the Faith of God.

Bahá'u'lláh laid down the foundation of a wonderful system of Administration so that individuals can organize the religious affairs of the community. This Administration enables all of us to work together for the progress of the Faith and the spiritual welfare of the community without the help of priests. The Bahá'í Administration and all the other institutions established by the teachings of Bahá'u'lláh are divine in origin. We shall read about it in the following pages.

What is Bahá'í Administration?

If there is a stretch of farmland with a river on one side of it, how would we distribute water to the various fields we wish to grow? We would first dig a canal that is large enough to bring sufficient water from the river to irrigate the whole area. Then we would dig smaller canals that would take water from the large canal to different sections of the land. Lastly, we would require a multitude of small channels to take water from these canals to every field. When our system of canals and streams is completed, the river will be able to irrigate all the farmland.

Bahá'í Administration, Shoghi Effendi has told us, is like a system of canals and streams "through which ... the Holy Spirit of the Cause pours forth" to the Bahá'í communities scattered throughout the world.[1]

In previous ages the priests were expected to bring the water of life from its Fountainhead to the people of the time. However, their power was limited. They could carry a handful of this water, and that too, only as long as they had the strength and the zeal to do so.

Bahá'u'lláh has not entrusted this task to individuals. He has planned a wonderful network of channels through which the water of life is brought to the field of existence. This plan is called the World Order of Bahá'u'lláh, and Bahá'í Administration is a part of it.

The good news of the World Order of Bahá'u'lláh was first proclaimed by the Báb when He said:

"Well is it with him who fixeth his gaze upon the Order of Bahá'u'lláh, and rendereth thanks unto his Lord. For He will assuredly be made manifest."[2]

Bahá'u'lláh laid the foundation for this World Order, and drafted its plan. 'Abdu'l-Bahá explained the details of the divine plan and started its construction. However, it was through the lifelong efforts of Shoghi Effendi that the Bahá'í Administration was gradually built up, and far-flung communities were joined to make them parts of a united whole.

Bahá'í Administration is different from every other form of religious order because it is not man-made. It is the Plan of God for this age, given to us through His Manifestation, Bahá'u'lláh, and destined to establish order and peace among all the various peoples of the earth.

---

1   Shoghi Effendi quoted in *Principles of Bahá'í Administration: A Compilation* (London: Bahá'í Publishing Trust, 1976), p. 1; and Shoghi Effendi: *Guidance for Today and Tomorrow* (London: Bahá'í Publishing Trust, 1953), p. 110).

2   The Báb quoted by Shoghi Effendi: *God Passes By*, pp. 25, 324–25; and *The World Order of Bahá'u'lláh*, pp. 146–47.

Bahá'í Administration is composed of many linked parts:

- Local Spiritual Assemblies (LSAs) elected by the Bahá'ís of their respective villages or towns. These act as the streams that bring water from the channels to the fields.
- National Spiritual Assemblies (NSAs) elected by the Bahá'ís of each country. These act as the channels that connect the streams to the one large canal into which water flows from the river itself.
- The Universal House of Justice elected by all the Bahá'ís of the world through their National Assemblies. It acts as the main canal. It is through the Universal House of Justice that God's guidance flows out to all parts of the world.

Before we cover the duties and responsibilities of each level of the Administration, let us make it quite clear that the Bahá'í Administration can never be divorced from Bahá'u'lláh's other teachings. No Bahá'í can believe in Bahá'u'lláh without accepting and working with His Administrative Order. It is an essential part of the Message of God that has been brought for the happiness of the individual, and most importantly, also for the unity and welfare of society. In some cases, the interests of the society have priority over those of individuals. However, it is in the best interests of society to foster the well-being of individuals.

As you can see from the following illustration, individuals within society are like the grains of corn in a field. A single grain of corn is of little significance. However, every grain of corn profits by the water that flows in for the benefit of the whole field.

We must realize that our individual happiness lies in the welfare of a united society and strive to strengthen this Administrative order on which depends the future hope of mankind. This is how we may illustrate our Administration:

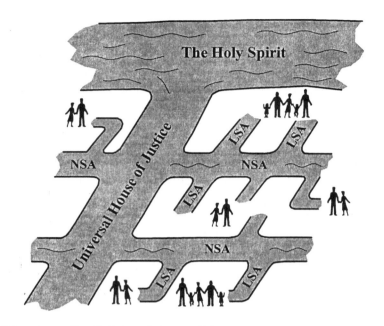

Election of a Spiritual Assembly

Bahá'u'lláh has ordained in the *Book of Aqdas*[1] that a Spiritual Assembly must be elected in every locality where the number of adult Bahá'ís is nine or more. This Spiritual Assembly, as a body, will serve the local community to which it belongs.

How do we elect our Local Spiritual Assembly?

Let us suppose that the Bahá'ís of Rampur[2], a village in India with about 60 believers, wish to elect their Spiritual Assembly. These are some of the points that they should remember:

1. They cannot form their Assembly at any time of the year. They can only elect their Assembly on the 21 April.[3] This

---

1   Bahá'u'lláh: *The Kitáb-i-Aqdas.*
2   A fictitious Indian village.
3   The anniversary of the Declaration of Bahá'u'lláh, the day on which He announced in the Garden of Ridván that He was the Promised One of all ages.

date is the first day of our Ridván festival and the only day
on which Bahá'ís can elect their Spiritual Assembly. If an
Assembly is not elected within the 24 hours between sunset
on the 20 April and sunset on the 21st, then the community
must wait a whole year until the next Ridván to elect their
Assembly.

2. Only Bahá'ís who are 21 years of age or over can vote for
    and be elected to the Spiritual Assembly. Let us use the
    community of 60 Bahá'ís living in Rampur as an example.
    There are 35 men and women who are either 21 or over that
    age. Only these 35 members can vote for their Assembly,
    and they must choose nine from among them to form their
    Assembly.

3. Every person who votes must write down the names of the
    nine persons whom he or she considers most worthy for
    being elected on the Spiritual Assembly. A vote is not valid
    if more or less than nine names are mentioned or if one
    name is repeated.

4. People should never be elected on the Spiritual Assembly
    because of their wealth or prestige in the community, or
    because they have shown kindness to us in some way and
    we wish to reward them. The only reason for selecting a
    person should be their sincerity and devotion to the Cause
    of God and their ability to serve the Faith. Every Bahá'í
    who can vote should consider the character and spiritual
    qualities of the men and women in his community. They
    should also pray to God that he may be guided to name the
    right people for the Assembly.

5. No Bahá'í is permitted to recommend anyone as worthy of
    membership of the Spiritual Assembly, no matter how good
    that person may be. Bahá'u'lláh has forbidden us to
    nominate any individual or try to draw attention to any
    special person before or during the election. No one in the
    Bahá'í community must know whom any other person has
    named, or intends to name, in his voting paper. Even a

husband and wife or close friends cannot consult together on whom they should choose. Every Bahá'í must seek assistance from God alone and make his own decisions in this matter without being influenced by the opinions of others. Only a Bahá'í who cannot write is allowed to ask a trusted person to write down the names that he or she dictates.

Keeping all these points in mind, the Bahá'ís of Rampur then elect the members of their Spiritual Assembly for that year. If they have all gathered at one place to give their votes, they will start their meeting with prayers asking God to help and bless them in their sacred task. Then the ballots will be collected, and a few Bahá'ís will be asked to count the votes. One person will read out the names written on each slip of paper, while two or three others will make a careful note of the number of votes received by each individual. The nine Bahá'ís who have received the largest number of votes are elected as members of the Local Spiritual Assembly for that year.

Thus the Bahá'ís of Rampur, like their fellow-believers in thousands of other villages, towns and cities in the East and the West, are blessed with a Spiritual Assembly that will serve their community until the first day of Ridván of the next year, then the process of election is once more repeated throughout the Bahá'í world.

Duties of a Local Spiritual Assembly

Regarding the duties of Spiritual Assemblies, Bahá'u'lláh has written:

"It behoveth them to be the trusted ones of the Merciful among men and to regard themselves as the guardians appointed of God for all that dwell on earth. It is incumbent upon them to take counsel together and to have regard for the interests of the servants of God, for His sake, even as they regard their own interests, and to choose that which is meet and seemly. Thus hath the Lord your God commanded you.

Beware lest ye put away that which is clearly revealed in His Tablet. Fear God, O ye that perceive.[1]

The Spiritual Assembly of every village or town must therefore guard the interests of the Bahá'ís in that locality.

The most important work of every Spiritual Assembly is to help Bahá'ís teach the Cause of God. The Message of Bahá'u'lláh is the source of blessings for all mankind, and our Spiritual Assemblies must become channels through which this great bounty can reach the people in every part of the world.

When you have formed your Spiritual Assembly, make sure that it takes up the matter of teaching as its main task.

Another important duty of a Spiritual Assembly is to try to promote amity and love among the believers. An Assembly must create a loving atmosphere of unity among the Bahá'ís; it must see that everybody is happy in that community. If there are any differences among the friends, it is the duty of the Spiritual Assembly to see that they are removed. Each Spiritual Assembly must act as a wise and loving father to the Bahá'ís of its locality.

Writing on the duties of Spiritual Assemblies, the Guardian says:

"They must do their utmost to extend at all times the helping hand to the poor, the sick, the disabled, the orphan, the widow, irrespective of colour, caste and creed."[2]

Every Spiritual Assembly has to have its own Fund. We will see how this Fund is to be collected by the voluntary contributions of friends, and how it is to be used in the interests of the Cause and the community. If the Bahá'ís enrich the Funds of their Assemblies, the Assemblies will, in turn, be able to

---

1 Bahá'u'lláh: *The Kitáb-i-Aqdas*, para. 30, p. 29.
2 Shoghi Effendi quoted in *Bahá'í Administration: Selected Messages 1922–33*, p. 38; and *Lights of Guidance*, p. 123.

come to the aid of the Bahá'ís when they are in need of assistance.

The education of Bahá'í children and youth is another responsibility of our Spiritual Assemblies. In the words of the beloved Guardian, "They must promote by every means in their power the material as well as the spiritual enlightenment of youth, the means for the education of children, institute, whenever possible, Bahá'í educational institutions, organize and supervise their work and provide the best means for their progress and development."[1]

Another important duty of the Spiritual Assemblies, according to the Guardian, is:

"They must undertake the arrangement of the regular meetings of the friends, the feasts and the anniversaries, as well as the special gatherings designed to serve and promote the social, intellectual and spiritual interests of their fellow-men."[2]

What we have mentioned above are some of the important functions of every Local Spiritual Assembly. Members of the Spiritual Assembly must be very careful in faithfully discharging their duties. They must always remember these Words of Bahá'u'lláh:

"It behoveth them to be the trusted ones of the Merciful among men ... and to have regard for the interests of the servants of God, for His sake ...."[3]

---

[1] Shoghi Effendi quoted in *Bahá'í Administration: Selected Messages 1922–33*, p. 38; and *Lights of Guidance*, p. 124.

[2] Shoghi Effendi quoted in *Bahá'í Administration: Selected Messages 1922–33*, p. 38.

[3] Bahá'u'lláh: *The Kitáb-i-Aqdas*, para. 30, p. 29; and *Bahá'í Administration: Selected Messages 1922–33*, p. 38.

Officers of the Spiritual Assembly

The members of a Spiritual Assembly are those nine Bahá'ís who receive more votes than the other Bahá'ís in their community on election day. After their election, the members of an Assembly must gather and hold their first meeting. Out of the nine elected members, the person receiving the highest number of votes is the temporary chairman. It is his duty to make arrangements for the members to quickly hold their first meeting.

They must begin their meetings with prayers to ask God to help them in promoting His Cause and to serve the community that has chosen them. After that, they must elect the officers of the Spiritual Assembly for that year.

Every Spiritual Assembly must have a Chairman, a Vice-Chairman, a Secretary and a Treasurer. This is necessary as it makes the work of the Assembly much easier.

The work of the Chairman is to conduct the meetings and help the Assembly to make decisions. If the members just gather to talk and disperse, then the Assembly will not accomplish anything. The Chairman asks for the views of all the members in every matter that comes up for discussion. Then he asks the members to vote on the subject to ensure that the Assembly makes a decision about the matters that it has considered. In the chapter on Consultation, we will read more about the decision making process.

The Vice-Chairman conducts the meetings of the Assembly whenever the Chairman is unable to attend, for example, in case of illness.

The Secretary is the person who keeps a record of all the work of the Assembly—all that has to be done and a record of what has been accomplished. The Secretary writes all the letters that have to be sent to individuals, to other Local Assemblies, or to the National Spiritual Assembly. It is through its Secretary that every Local Assembly is in touch with the rest of the Bahá'í World.

The Treasurer is in charge of the Assembly Fund. He gives receipts to all who contribute to the Fund and pays out from this amount the expenses undertaken by the Spiritual Assembly.

When electing the officers of the Assembly, the members must consider the merits of each individual and determine which one is most capable of performing the duties assigned to these different officers. The same principles that had been used for the election of the members of the Assembly should now be applied in electing its officers. This election, therefore, is also to be carried out by secret ballot, and without any electioneering. No one should be elected because of his or her social standing. Let us assume that among the members of the Assembly there is an elderly and highly respected member of the community. This respect or his age are not reasons for electing him as the Chairman of the Spiritual Assembly. A good reason would be if he is the most capable person of undertaking this duty. The same is true of a person whose wealth may give him a social position.

On the other hand, we must also remember that the officers of the Spiritual Assembly have no special position in the community. The Chairman, for instance, is not the leader of the community nor the most respected personality. His or her station outside a Spiritual Assembly meeting is the same as that of any other member of the community. When the meeting of the Assembly is over, he or she has no more rights in the community than any other Bahá'í.

To make the point quite clear, let us think of the people of a village who need pure drinking water and decide to dig a well. The headman in that village, though highly respected, may have no knowledge of how to dig a well. However, there may be a young man, with no special position in the village, who has had considerable experience in this matter. Which of these two men would the villagers choose to execute the job? It is the young man who will be entrusted with the work, and the headman of the village may be the first one to choose him for this purpose.

While working on the well, all the villagers—even the headman himself—will accept the guidance of the young man that they themselves have chosen to supervise the work. This does not mean, of course, that the young man is going to become the leader of the village in everything or that the headman is going to lose his position in the community. It is this spirit of co-operation that will benefit everybody in the village.

It is with this spirit of loving co-operation and harmony that the Bahá'ís elect their Spiritual Assembly and the Spiritual Assembly elects its officers.

The beloved Guardian wrote that the members of a Spiritual Assembly "... *should approach their task with extreme humility, and endeavour, by their open-mindedness, their high sense of justice and duty, their candour, their modesty, their entire devotion to the welfare and interests of the friends, the Cause, and humanity, to win, not only the confidence and the genuine support and respect of those whom they serve, but also their esteem and real affection.*"[1]

The Spiritual Assembly at work—Part I

Let us suppose that the village of Rampur has elected its Local Spiritual Assembly, and Babulal has received more votes than the other eight members. What happens next? Babulal invites all the other members to gather at a special hour in one place to hold their first meeting. They decide to meet an hour after sunset on 22 April, the second day of the Feast of Riḍván, in the village square. We will follow them there to see what they will do.

Babulal arrives a little before the appointed time. He has brought his lamp with him in case their meeting should continue until after dark. The other members now start arriving from their work in the fields. They greet each other and go to the

---

1 Shoghi Effendi quoted in *Bahá'í Administration: Selected Messages 1922–33*, p. 64; and *Lights of Guidance*, pp. 32–33.

village well for a wash. After having cleaned and refreshed themselves, they gather on a platform in the village square. At exactly an hour after sunset, Babulal announces that the Assembly will start its work.

A few prayers are first said by two or three of the members— this gives their meeting a wonderful spiritual atmosphere. Then Babulal says that they must elect the Chairman of the Assembly. He cuts a sheet of paper into small pieces and, giving each member one piece, requests them to write down the name of the person whom they consider most suited among themselves to be Chairman of their Assembly.

Five members of the Assembly cannot write; so Babulal asks one of the members to go to each of these in turn, and write down the name of the person they want to elect as Chairman. The nine pieces of paper are then collected and mixed together in such a way that no one can tell to whom each belongs. Then Babulal asks two other members to help him count the votes. While he himself reads them out one by one, the other two make a note of the names on the paper, and then count them to see which member has received more votes than all the others.

Lal Chand has received five votes, Babulal three votes and Kamla one vote. Therefore, Lal Chand is elected as the Chairman of the Assembly. If no one had received more than four votes, then they would have to repeat this election because the officers of the Assembly must each receive at least five votes before being elected. The election is repeated until someone does get the required number of votes.

Now that Lal Chand has been chosen as Chairman, it is his duty to supervise the election of the rest of the Assembly's officers. After thanking Babulal for having done his part, Lal Chand now hands out pieces of paper on which all the members must now vote for their Vice-Chairman. The same procedure that was followed for the election of the Chairman is now repeated in electing all the other officers of the Assembly.

The result of the election is that: Mrs Shanta Devi is elected as Vice-Chairman, Babulal as Secretary and Ḥasan-'Alí as Treasurer of the Local Spiritual Assembly of Rampur.

The Chairman then asks the Secretary to record the minutes, that is, make notes on what has been done during the first meeting of the Assembly.

By this time it is quite late, and one of the members suggests that they adjourn the meeting and come together again the next day. All agree to this proposal, and it is decided to hold their next meeting on the morrow at the same time and at the same place. The meeting is closed with a prayer, as every Bahá'í gathering should be, and the members of the Assembly go to their homes.

We shall read about their second meeting in the coming pages.

Consultation

Bahá'í Administration works through consultation. Consultation is applied to Bahá'í work in the Nineteen Day Feast, the Local Spiritual Assembly meetings, the Bahá'í Convention, the National Spiritual Assembly meetings, and in our Committee meetings and conferences. The Guardian tells us to remember two important virtues when we are consulting in Bahá'í gatherings—truthfulness and frankness.[1]

While we come together in a Bahá'í meeting, we must always feel that Bahá'u'lláh is with us in spirit. This creates a wonderful spiritual atmosphere that helps us in our consultations. If we feel the presence of Bahá'u'lláh in our meetings, then we will always try to be worthy servants of His Cause, whether we are serving on an Assembly, a Committee or

---

1 Shoghi Effendi quoted in *Bahá'í Administration: Selected Messages 1922–33*, p. 102; *Lights of Guidance*, p. 180; and *The Compilation of Compilations*, Vol. II (Trustworthiness), pp. 347–48.

a Nineteen Day Feast. We will make every effort to suppress selfish motives or unfair statements during consultations; no trace of insincerity will find its way into our discussions; and nothing but the truth will be spoken, for Bahá'u'lláh has said:

> *"O HEEDLESS ONES!*
>
> *"Think not the secrets of hearts are hidden, nay, know ye of a certainty that in clear characters they are engraved and are openly manifest in the holy Presence."*[1]

In Bahá'í consultation, everybody should express his views with absolute freedom. He should only think of the interests of the Cause, and forget his personal relationships with the other individuals present. For example, if a father and a son are both members of an Assembly, then at the time of consultation or of giving votes, the son should not consider it his duty to agree with his father. Bahá'ís are commanded to have the greatest respect for their parents. However, when they are taking part in a Bahá'í consultation, they must remember that they are responsible only to Bahá'u'lláh Who is present in their meeting and Whose Cause they are serving. They should never let personal feelings interfere with the interests of the Faith. Therefore, if the son feels that his father's views are wrong, it is his duty to say so. In addition, the father should not expect his son to do otherwise, because he knows that they have both come to the meeting to serve the Cause with absolute honesty. Neither is expected to please the other with their views.

Let us beware lest petty personal grudges creep into our hearts at the time of consultation and influence our views. If, for instance, an acquaintance of mine has not assisted me when I asked him to do something for me, then I should take great care that this incident does not prejudice my views against some good suggestion that that person may have in the meeting. Here again, I must remember the presence of Bahá'u'lláh, and let

---

[1] Bahá'u'lláh: *The Hidden Words of Bahá'u'lláh*, (Persian) No. 59.

nothing come in the way of service to His Cause. When Bahá'ís come together in a meeting, they should work as *"fingers of one hand"*[1] and *"drops of one ocean"*.[2]

We should never insist on our views, or try to impose our will on others. We have all seen how two small children sometimes quarrel, each one insisting that he is right and the other is wrong. They may continue to quarrel in this way for a long time without achieving anything. However, when their father comes, they lower their raised voices through love and respect for him, and soon their problem is solved in his presence. If we know that Bahá'u'lláh is with us at every meeting, then we will never act in a manner that is unworthy in His presence.

Although every Bahá'í is free to express his opinion in consultations, the decision that is arrived at depends on the wisdom of the majority of the members. Once a decision has been taken, every Bahá'í must respect it, even those who had different views themselves. Let us suppose that Shyam is a member of the Spiritual Assembly and suggests that the meeting for the Feast of the 12th day of Riḍván be held on the morning of the 2 May. However, the majority of the members vote for the Bahá'ís to gather after sunset on 1 May. Now Shyam might have had very good reasons for his suggestion. However, once the Assembly has decided against it, Shyam must put aside his own view, accept the decision of the Assembly with all his heart, and try his best in helping to arrange for the meeting after sunset.

'Abdu'l-Bahá has said:

"In this day, assemblies of consultation are of the greatest importance and a vital necessity. Obedience unto them is essential and obligatory. The members thereof must take

1   Bahá'u'lláh: *The Kitáb-i-Aqdas*, para. 58, p. 40; *Gleanings from the Writings of Bahá'u'lláh*, p. 140; and *The Proclamation of Bahá'u'lláh*, 118.
2   Bahá'u'lláh: *The Kitáb-i-Aqdas*, Other Sections, p. 92; and *Tablets of Bahá'u'lláh*, pp. 27, 128.

counsel together in such wise that no occasion for ill-feeling or discord may arise. This can be attained when every member expresseth with absolute freedom his own opinion and setteth forth his argument. Should anyone oppose, he must on no account feel hurt for not until matters are fully discussed can the right way be revealed. The shining spark of truth cometh forth only after the clash of differing opinions. If after discussion, a decision be carried unanimously, well and good; but if, the Lord forbid, differences of opinion should arise, a majority of voices must prevail."[1]

The different views offered by the members of an Assembly are like the different ingredients of a delicious stew. When we want to make a good stew, we mix many different ingredients together and boil it until it is well cooked. It is delicious only when the ingredients are well blended, for each contributes to the taste of the stew. However, if we were to taste those ingredients separately, they would never taste so good. Similarly, every individual opinion offered by the Bahá'ís gathered in a meeting contributes something towards the ultimate decision that is taken. The decision itself is not one person's opinion. It is not just the sum of the views of all the members. It is based on the collective wisdom of an Assembly.

In the following Tablet, 'Abdu'l-Bahá clearly shows the way Bahá'ís should consult together. Let us read it carefully and follow it in our meetings:

"The prime requisites for them that take counsel together are purity of motive, radiance of spirit, detachment from all else save God, attraction to His Divine Fragrances, humility and lowliness amongst His loved ones, patience and long-suffering in difficulties and servitude to His exalted Threshold. Should they be graciously aided to acquire these

---

1   'Abdu'l-Bahá quoted in *Bahá'í Administration: Selected Messages 1922–33*, p. 21; and Shoghi Effendi: *Unfolding Destiny*, p. 6.

attributes, victory from the unseen Kingdom of Bahá shall be vouchsafed to them.

"... The first condition is absolute love and harmony amongst the members of the assembly. They must be wholly free from estrangement and must manifest in themselves the Unity of God, for they are the waves of one sea, the drops of one river, the stars of one heaven, the rays of one sun, the trees of one orchard, the flowers of one garden. Should harmony of thought and absolute unity be non-existent, that gathering shall be dispersed and that assembly be brought to naught. ... They must, when coming together, turn their faces to the Kingdom on High and ask aid from the Realm of Glory. They must then proceed with the utmost devotion, courtesy, dignity, care and moderation to express their views. They must in every matter search out the truth and not insist upon their own opinion, for stubbornness and persistence in one's views will lead ultimately to discord and wrangling and the truth will remain hidden. The honoured members must with all freedom express their own thoughts, and it is in no wise permissible for one to belittle the thought of another, nay, he must with moderation set forth the truth, and should differences of opinion arise a majority of voices must prevail, and all must obey and submit to the majority. It is again not permitted that any one of the honoured members object to or censure, whether in or out of the meeting, any decision arrived at previously, though that decision be not right, for such criticism would prevent any decision from being enforced. In short, whatsoever thing is arranged in harmony and with love and purity of motive, its result is light, and should the least trace of estrangement prevail the result shall be darkness upon darkness. ... If this be so regarded, that assembly shall be of God, but otherwise it shall lead to coolness and alienation that proceed from the Evil One."[1]

---

1   'Abdu'l-Bahá: *Selections from the Writings of 'Abdu'l-Bahá*, pp. 87–88. Quoted in *Bahá'í Administration: Selected Messages 1922–33*, pp. 21–22; and Shoghi Effendi: *Unfolding Destiny*, pp. 6–7.

"Discussions must all be confined to spiritual matters that pertain to the training of souls, the instruction of children, the relief of the poor, the help of the feeble throughout all classes in the world, kindness to all peoples, the diffusion of the fragrances of God and the exaltation of His Holy Word. Should they endeavour to fulfil these conditions the Grace of the Holy Spirit shall be vouchsafed until them, and that assembly shall become the centre of the Divine blessings, the hosts of Divine confirmation shall come to their aid, and they shall day by day receive a new effusion of Spirit."[1]

The Spiritual Assembly at work—Part II

The nine members of the Spiritual Assembly of Rampur met again on 23 April. The Chairman asked some of the members to say a few prayers. These were prayers by Bahá'u'lláh and 'Abdu'l-Bahá, some of them written especially for reading in meetings. After the opening prayers, the Chairman asked the Secretary to read the minutes of the previous meeting from the notes he had recorded. This is what the Secretary read:

"The first meeting of the Spiritual Assembly of Rampur was held on the 22 April, an hour, after sunset. Opening prayers were read and Mr Babulal conducted the first part of the meeting. Election of the Chairman took place; Mr Lal Chand was elected Chairman, and therefore conducted the rest of the meeting. The election of the officers of the Assembly was continued, and the following members were elected:

"Mrs Shanti Devi, Vice-Chairman; Mr Ḥasan-'Alí, Treasurer and Mr Babulal, Secretary.

"It was decided to hold the next meeting of the assembly on the 23 April. The meeting adjourned with a closing prayer, three hours after sunset."

---

[1]   'Abdu'l-Bahá quoted in *The Compilation of Compilations*, (The Local Spiritual Assembly) Vol. II, p. 47; *Bahá'í Administration: Selected Messages 1922–33*, pp. 22–23; and Shoghi Effendi: *Unfolding Destiny*, pp. 7–8.

When the Secretary finished reading, the Chairman asked the other members if they approved the minutes of their last meeting. Everybody agreed that the minutes were correct, and Babulal noted down that the minutes of the last meeting had been read and approved.

The Chairman then announced that as the main purpose of every Spiritual Assembly was to spread the Message of God, they would like to discuss this matter in their meeting.

The Chairman invited each member to express his views on this subject. When they had all given their views, the Chairman summarized them as follows:

1. We ourselves need to know more about the Cause.
2. We need literature.
3. We need a fund.
4. We have to start our teaching activities in the neighbouring villages.

Then they looked at these subjects one by one. One of the members suggested that they tell the community about this important undertaking to see if anybody could participate in the teaching campaign that they were going to start. One member suggested that to know more about the Cause they would need to have weekly meetings to study the Cause. They could use their Saturday meetings for this purpose. He suggested that they ask Sunil, who was the teacher in the Bahá'í School of the neighbouring village, to conduct the classes.

The Chairman asked who seconded this proposal. Ameeta seconded it. After a little discussion, the Chairman put the suggestion to a vote. He asked those who approved of the suggestion, to call Sunil from the village of Gandhinagar to conduct their Saturday classes, to raise their hands.

Seven members raised their hands. The other two members, Amrik and Lal Chand, who thought that Sunil would not be able travel such a long distance, did not agree with the proposal and did not raise their hands.

The Chairman announced that the suggestion was carried and asked the Secretary to record the decision in the minutes.

Then the Chairman announced that Sunil, the teacher, has to travel by bus to reach their village and he must leave his part-time job that he was doing in the evening in his village. Therefore, a Fund had to be raised to help Sunil to reach Rampur to conduct the classes. The Chairman asked the others what they thought about this idea. Amrik said, "We, the members of the Assembly, must set an example of devotion to our Faith for the rest of community. I promise to pay one day's wages to the Fund every month. I will be glad to offer it to the Assembly." This made all the members very happy and they congratulated Amrik for his generous donation to the community. They were particularly happy that though Amrik originally did not vote for the suggestion, now that it had been passed by the Local Spiritual Assembly, he lent his support to it. When an Assembly passes a resolution, whether we agree with it or not, we must accept and respect the vote of the majority. The other members of the Local Spiritual Assembly also contributed some money. Their names and the amounts promised by them were noted by the Secretary. The Treasurer also made a note of these contributions and announced that 200 rupees (Rs) per month were promised by the members of the Assembly for the Fund.

It was decided to announce this decision to the community at the Nineteen Day Feast, to be held on 28 April (Feast of Beauty), and to ask the friends for their support of this activity.

The Chairman then reverted to the question of literature required for their teaching activities. After discussion, the Assembly decided to ask the National Spiritual Assembly for their assistance.

After these arrangements were made the Chairman announced that the question they must next discuss was how to start spreading the Faith in the neighbouring villages.

Babulal proposed that every Sunday groups of Bahá'ís should visit the villages around Rampur. Others also agreed with this suggestion. Another member added that Sunday would be the most suitable day because on Saturday they would have their study class and then Sunil could also accompany them in their teaching tours on Sunday.

Babulal, the Secretary, noted these ideas.

The Chairman asked if there were any more suggestions on the subject.

Ḥasan-'Alí said that it was a good idea to hold large public meetings on special Holy Days and anniversaries, and to invite non-Bahá'í friends and relatives from nearby places to these meetings.

This suggestion was seconded, put to the vote, and approved by the Assembly.

A number of decisions were made. To present the Assembly's plans to the community at the next Nineteen Day Feast. Ask the Bahá'ís of Rampur to help with the Assembly Fund. Ask for volunteers for teaching activities to neighbouring villages.

Lastly, they decided that the next meeting of the Assembly would take place on 29 April—one day after the Nineteen Day Feast so that the suggestions made by the community during the Feast could be discussed by the Assembly.

After a closing prayer, the members of the Assembly went home with joyful hearts thanking God for having assisted them in arriving at such vital decisions for the good of the community

What took place in this meeting is an example of how a Spiritual Assembly should conduct its work, how it should enter into discussions, and how it should arrive at useful decisions. The problems that occur in different communities may not be the same, and even their needs may not be alike. Every Assembly should carefully consider its duties and decide to consult on its tasks according to their importance in each community.

The Spiritual Assembly at work—Part III
The Nineteen Day Feast

It is the Feast of Beauty (Jamál) and the Bahá'ís of Rampur have gathered for their Nineteen Day Feast. The Chairman of the Assembly conducts all the meetings of the Nineteen Day Feasts unless he is unable to attend, in which case the Vice-Chairman takes his place. The first part of the Feast is always given to prayers and readings from the Writings of the Báb, Bahá'u'lláh and 'Abdu'l-Bahá. These can be read by any of the Bahá'ís present in the gathering at the request of the Chairman, while all listen to the Words with great care and attention. The number of prayers and readings must not be so many as to make everybody tired.

When the Bahá'ís of Rampur finished the first part of the programme, the Chairman of their Spiritual Assembly, Lal Chand, asked the Secretary, Babulal, to read the report of the Assembly. Babulal told the community the names of the elected officers of the Assembly and the Assembly's decision to start a teaching campaign for spreading the Message of God in the neighbouring area. He also told the community of the assistance needed in the teaching work and the funds that were required to invite a teacher and hold conferences.

After the report of the Secretary, the Chairman asked the members of the community for their suggestions on these matters and how they were able to help. Each of the Bahá'ís promised to help in one way or another. One said that he could supply a pound of wheat at each conference. Another said he would pay the one-way fare of the teacher once in a month, while a third promised to dedicate one full day each week to teaching activities. Besides these promises of co-operation, the Bahá'ís of Rampur drew the attention of their Assembly to some very important facts that they had not considered. For example, besides the weekly study classes and teaching tours, they might also make preparations to give the Message at country fairs that were being held from time to time. Those who were going to these fairs should also take Bahá'í literature with them for distribution. Many valuable suggestions were also given on methods to economize on the use of the funds, etc. The Secretary noted all the suggestions made at the Nineteen Day Feast so that the Spiritual Assembly might consider them at its next session.

The Chairman promised that the Spiritual Assembly would carefully consider all the Feast suggestions and communicate the results of its decisions to the community at the next Nineteen Day Feast.

The third part of the programme of the Nineteen Day Feast is the entertainment period. Four of the Bahá'í families in Rampur shared the task of providing some puffed rice to be served to everyone. A group of young people sang some beautiful songs and many of the others joined them in the chorus. A Bahá'í girl recited a lovely poem that she had memorized at school.

The spirit of unity and happiness with which the Bahá'ís of Rampur held their Nineteen Day Feast brought spiritual blessings that were felt by all. They left the meeting after a closing prayer, and took their happiness with them into their homes.

Some Points on the Nineteen Day Feast

One of the duties of every Assembly is to see that the friends of its locality observe the Nineteen Day Feasts once every nineteen days by the Bahá'ís of every town or village. The holding of regular community Feasts is very important as it *"... was inaugurated by the Báb and ratified by Bahá'u'lláh ...."*[1].

Question: What is the purpose of a Nineteen Day Feast?

Answer: 'Abdu'l-Bahá says that in the Nineteen Day Feast

---

1 'Abdu'l-Bahá: *The Compilation of Compilations*, (The Nineteen Day Feast) Vol. I, p. 430.

"... people may gather together and outwardly show fellowship and love, that the divine mysteries may be disclosed. The object is concord, that through this fellowship hearts may become perfectly united, and reciprocity and mutual helpfulness be established."[1]

Question: What should we do at the Nineteen Day Feast?

Answer: This feast is a part of the Bahá'í Administration and as the beloved Guardian has explained, the programme of the Nineteen Day Feast consists of three parts. The first part is a devotional programme. Prayers and readings from the Holy Writings may be offered by a few friends at the beginning of the Feast. The second part is administrative. The Spiritual Assembly through its Secretary gives reports of its activities and asks the Bahá'í friends of the locality to give their suggestions and pledges for the promotion of the Cause of Bahá'u'lláh. The period of consultation is the time for the believers to voice proposals to be sent through the Local Spiritual Assembly to the National Spiritual Assembly. The third part is entertainment. Songs may be sung by the friends, stories may be told, etc. Refreshments, no matter how simple, are served.

Question: Who invites people to the Feast?

Answer: Where there is an Assembly, the Secretary invites the Bahá'ís according to the dates given in the Bahá'í calendar to a particular place at a specific time. In a locality where there is no Assembly, the Bahá'ís may form a group and elect a person from among themselves as the Secretary of the Group. This Secretary will remind the Bahá'í community about the Nineteen Day Feasts.

Question: Who conducts the Nineteen Day Feast?

Answer: Chairman of the Assembly conducts the Nineteen Day Feast. He will ask individuals to chant prayers at the

---

1   'Abdu'l-Bahá: *The Compilation of Compilations*, (The Nineteen Day Feast) Vol. I, p. 430.

beginning and later request friends to consult with the Assembly during the second part.

Question: Who plays host to the Feast?

Answer: Individual Bahá'ís usually play host at the Feast, each taking a turn. Sometimes the Assembly observes the Nineteen Day Feast by using its own funds. It is also possible that a few Bahá'ís may combine to be the host of a Feast. It is preferable that the physical feast should consist of some simple food or snacks. However, this is not necessary as Bahá'u'lláh says that even by serving plain water we can be the host of the Nineteen Day Feast. The most important aspects of the Nineteen Day Feast are the spiritual development of the Bahá'ís and the unity and harmony among them. It should also serve to assist the progress of the Cause in the locality through consultation and collaboration with the Spiritual Assembly.

We quote below from the Writings of 'Abdu'l-Bahá to show the spirit of every Bahá'í meeting:

"In these meetings outside conversation must be entirely avoided, and the gathering must be confined to chanting the verses and reading the Words, and to matters which concern the Cause of God, such as explaining proofs, adducing clear and manifest evidences, and tracing the signs of the Beloved One of the creatures. Those who attend the meeting must, before entering, be arrayed with the utmost cleanliness and turn to the Abhá Kingdom, and then enter the meeting with all meekness and humbleness; and while the Tablets are being read, must be quiet and silent; and if one wishes to speak he must do so with all courtesy, with the satisfaction and permission of those present, and do it with eloquence and fluency."[1]

---

1 'Abdu'l-Bahá quoted by J. E. Esselmont: *Bahá'u'lláh and the New Era,* Chapter 11, Meetings section, p. 172.

The dates of holding the Feasts are as follows:

First Day	Arabic Name	Translation
21 March	Bahá	Splendour
9 April	Jalál	Glory
28 April	Jamál	Beauty
17 May	'Aẓamat	Grandeur
5 June	Núr	Light
24 June	Raḥmat	Mercy
13 July	Kalimát	Words
1 August	Kamál	Perfection
20 August	Asmá'	Names
8 September	'Izzat	Might
27 September	Mashíyyat	Will
16 October	'Ilm	Knowledge
4 November	Qudrat	Power
23 November	Qawl	Speech
12 December	Masá'il	Questions
31 December	Sharaf	Honour
19 January	Sulṭán	Sovereignty
7 February	Mulk	Dominion
2 March	'Alá'	Loftiness

The Spiritual Assembly of Rampur met on the day after the Nineteen Day Feast. The minutes of their previous meeting were first read and approved before they discussed the suggestions given by the community at the last Feast. After careful consideration, they approved all the suggestions except one.

The Assembly decided to invite all the Bahá'ís to a picnic on the last day of Riḍván. They also decided to inform the friends which group they were placed in to visit the various neighbouring villages for teaching activities. Three of the members of the Assembly were chosen to form a committee to arrange a suitable programme for the meeting that was to take place on the last day of Riḍván.

Before closing the meeting of the Assembly, there was one other matter to discuss. Two of the members had requested assistance of the Assembly to help them solve a personal difficulty that had arisen between them and on which they had not been able to agree. The Assembly listened to what each side had to say, and then proposed a solution for their problem in a spirit of great love and wisdom.

When the Secretary of the Assembly consulted his notes the next day, he wrote the following letter to the National Spiritual Assembly:

The Secretary,
National Spiritual Assembly,
New Delhi.

Dear Bahá'í Friends,

We are glad to inform you that by the grace of Bahá'u'lláh we have formed our Spiritual Assembly in Rampur. We have already returned the forms that you asked us to fill out after the election, giving the names and addresses of the members and officers of the Assembly.

We have requested Mr Sunil, the Bahá'í teacher of Gandhinagar, to come every Saturday to our village to conduct weekly study meetings.

We have decided that on every Sunday a number of the friends would go to the neighbouring villages to teach the Cause among new areas.

We have raised a special Fund to which the friends have so far contributed Rs 145, with promises of contributions of the same amount every month. This amount will be spent on teaching activities under the supervision of this Assembly.

As we lack a sufficient quantity of literature, we request the National Assembly's help in sending this Assembly a large number of pamphlets and declaration cards.

We hope to be able to write to you soon of the good news of the progress of the Cause in our next letter.

May Bahá'u'lláh assist us in His service!

Yours sincerely,
BABULAL
Secretary

National Spiritual Assembly

All the Local Spiritual Assemblies in our country are linked through a National Spiritual Assembly.

The National Spiritual Assembly is a body that is elected by the Bahá'ís of the country through a National Convention. Delegates are sent to this Convention from all parts of that country. The basic rules of Bahá'í elections, which have been mentioned before, apply to the election of the National Spiritual Assembly too. Bahá'í elections are a sacred duty that takes on a spiritual character; no prior nominations nor propaganda are ever used.

The purpose of a National Spiritual Assembly is to guide, co-ordinate and unite the work that is done by the Bahá'ís throughout the country and to encourage them in their activities. Bahá'í communities lend their co-operation to the National Spiritual Assembly through their Local Spiritual Assemblies. The National Spiritual Assembly maintains contact with the Bahá'ís of the country through letters and circulars. It provides them with news about the activities of other Bahá'ís and the progress of the Faith throughout the world. The National Spiritual Assembly also asks the Bahá'ís for their suggestions, invites them to consultations, and expects their co-operation in implementing the Assembly's decisions.

The circulars of the National Spiritual Assembly are read by the Secretaries of the Local Spiritual Assemblies at the Nineteen Day Feasts. If they call for consultation, then every individual Bahá'í is welcome to give his views or promise of co-operation. The result of these consultations at the Nineteen Day Feasts will be sent to the National Spiritual Assembly by the Local Spiritual Assembly of each locality. The National Spiritual Assembly will then go through all these suggestions and decide what action should be taken after careful deliberation.

If a locality has fewer than nine adult Bahá'ís,[1] then the National Spiritual Assembly writes to the person who has been chosen by the group to act as Secretary. When there is only one Bahá'í in a locality, then the National Spiritual Assembly corresponds with him directly.

As the National Spiritual Assembly has many duties, it appoints committees to help it with their work. The members who are to serve on these committees are chosen by the National Spiritual Assembly itself, and a special task is given to each committee. If, for example, the National Spiritual Assembly of India decides to build a House of Worship in the country, it will appoint a special committee to see to all the details of the work and give suggestions for the construction of the Temple. The National Spiritual Assembly is free to accept the suggestions of the committee; to modify or even to reject them. Local Spiritual Assemblies can also appoint committees in the same way to assist them where they feel it is necessary. The committees that are appointed by the National Spiritual Assembly or by Local Spiritual Assemblies are directly responsible to the Assembly for which they are working. The Local Spiritual Assemblies are responsible to the National Spiritual Assembly, and the National Spiritual Assembly is the highest authority for the Bahá'ís in every country.

---

1   A community with less than nine adults Bahá'ís cannot elect a Local Spiritual Assembly. They are often described as a Bahá'í Group.

The National Spiritual Assembly, like the Local Spiritual Assembly, elects a Chairman, a Vice-Chairman, a Treasurer and a Secretary. The duties of the officers in the National Spiritual Assembly are the same as those of the officers of a Local Spiritual Assembly but at a national level.

National Convention

The members of a National Spiritual Assembly are elected each year by delegates chosen to represent regional areas. This means that each Bahá'í community or electoral unit elects a certain number of delegates from its own members. These delegates meet annually at a National Convention where they elect the members of the National Spiritual Assembly.

The number of delegates that are elected in each locality depends upon the number of Bahá'ís in that region. The National Spiritual Assembly of every country designates the extent of each region and the number of delegates to represent each region.

The delegates to the Convention will travel from all parts of the country to gather at one place, sometime during the 12 days of Riḍván (21 April to 2 May). The preferred meeting place will be at the National Spiritual Assembly's office. The main purpose of the Convention is to elect the members of the National Spiritual Assembly for that year. Another important task for the delegates is to consult with the new National Spiritual Assembly and with each other about the progress of the Cause in the country.

After the Convention is opened with a few prayers, the members elect a Chairman for their meetings. The duty of the Chairman, here too, is to see that the consultations are carried out in an orderly manner and with the Bahá'í spirit. The members of the Convention then elect a Secretary to record the suggestions that they wish to offer to the National Spiritual Assembly.

Here are a few important points that we must know about the Convention:

1. Delegates to the Convention must elect the members of the National Spiritual Assembly from among the Bahá'ís of the whole country. The selection of members is not limited to the Convention delegates. They can choose any nine adults (21 years and older) belonging to the entire Bahá'í community of the country.

2. Those who are elected as delegates to the Convention have neither duties nor privileges other than their participation in the Convention and the election of the new National Spiritual Assembly. The duties of the delegates end when the Convention is over, unless a vacancy arises on the National Spiritual Assembly during the year. In that case, the delegates are called upon to vote in a by-election. Hence, a Convention is not a permanent body, and there can be no permanent members after the Convention has ended.

3. The Convention is a consultative body. Its recommendations are passed on to the National Spiritual Assembly and the Assembly is free to accept or reject those recommendations.

4. The Convention has no supremacy over the National Spiritual Assembly. The National Spiritual Assembly is the highest authority in each country and has control over all Local Spiritual Assemblies and individual Bahá'ís in the country.

The Universal House of Justice

One of the unique institutions of the Bahá'í Faith is the Universal House of Justice whose members are elected from amongst the Bahá'ís of the whole world through their National Spiritual Assemblies. Bahá'u'lláh has assured us that He will continue to guide the Bahá'ís through the Universal House of Justice as long as the Bahá'í Dispensation lasts.

Bahá'u'lláh has given us the fundamental laws and teachings of God for this age. However, He has said that we shall also need other social rules that will be gradually decided for us according to our changing needs. These social rules and regulations, Bahá'u'lláh says, must be ordained by the Universal House of Justice that will always be under the unerring guidance of God.

About the Universal House of Justice, 'Abdu'l-Bahá says:

"... if it be established under the necessary conditions—with members elected from all the people—that House of Justice will be under the protection and the unerring guidance of God. If that House of Justice shall decide unanimously, or by a majority, upon any question not mentioned in the Book, that decision and command will be guarded from mistake."[1]

It is, therefore, obvious that the Universal House of Justice will be inspired in all its decisions, and that whatever rules it may ordain, will be perfect for the requirements of the times. However, we must not think that the House of Justice will ever change those fundamental principles that have been given us by Bahá'u'lláh. What it will do is to set the rules by which we must carry out the laws of Bahá'u'lláh. For instance, one of the principles of the Bahá'í Faith is that there should be no extremes of wealth or poverty in the world. However, Bahá'u'lláh has not told us how much tax people should pay. It is left to the Universal House of Justice to work out a method of taxation that will enable everyone to live a comfortable life, and at the same time prevent anyone from accumulating excessive wealth.

Another example is that Bahá'u'lláh has commanded us to have a universal language in the world, but he has not mentioned which language it should be. This again has been left to the Universal House of Justice to decide.

In this connection Bahá'u'lláh writes:

---

[1]   'Abdu'l-Bahá: *Some Answered Questions*, p. 172; and quoted in *Lights of Guidance*, No. 1065, p. 317.

"In former Epistles We have enjoined upon the Trustees of the House of Justice either to choose one language from among those now existing or to adopt a new one, and in like manner to select a common script, both of which should be taught in all the schools of the world."[1]

Although the Universal House of Justice cannot change anything that has been revealed by Bahá'u'lláh, or alter any of the interpretations of 'Abdu'l-Bahá and Shoghi Effendi, it can change its own decisions if circumstances require it. Suppose the Universal House of Justice, at one time, chooses a set of tax rates. That decision is no doubt perfect for that time, but fifty years later it may no longer suit the requirements of the time. The Universal House of Justice, therefore, is free to change their previous decision.

In His *Will and Testament* 'Abdu'l-Bahá writes:

"Unto the Most Holy Book everyone must turn, and all that is not expressly recorded therein must be referred to the Universal House of Justice. That which this body, whether unanimously or by a majority doth carry, that is verily the truth and the purpose of God Himself. Whoso doth deviate therefrom is verily of them that love discord, hath shown forth malice, and turned away from the Lord of the Covenant."[2]

The labours of our beloved Guardian, during the thirty–six years of his ministry, paved the way for the establishment of the Universal House of Justice. The Guardian mentioned that the Universal House of Justice was like the dome of a building that needed strong pillars to support it. Those pillars, he said, were the National Spiritual Assemblies of the world. And it was through the ceaseless efforts of our Guardian that these pillars were erected one by one in all parts of the earth. Under the divine guidance of the Guardian, Bahá'ís learned to work

---

1   Bahá'u'lláh: *Tablets of Bahá'u'lláh*, p. 127.
2   'Abdu'l-Bahá: *Will and Testament*, pp. 19–20.

together in groups and Local Assemblies, and later, in each country, through their National Spiritual Assembly. Then he gave them the Ten Year Plan that taught the National Spiritual Assemblies to work together on a world undertaking. The Plan also helped the Bahá'ís to establish the additional pillars of the Universal House of Justice. By the end of the Ten Year Plan in 1963, there were sufficient National Spiritual Assemblies throughout the world to establish the Universal House of Justice.

'Abdu'l-Bahá foretold that the Universal House of Justice would be formed when the Bahá'í Faith had spread to all parts of the world. This occurred at the end of the Ten Year Plan—in April 1963.

Some Important Points about the Bahá'í Administration

1.   Obedience to the decisions of the Assembly.

A Bahá'í Spiritual Assembly should be regarded by the Bahá'ís as a sacred institution because it is based on the Teachings of God.   We must therefore obey all the decisions of the Assembly. 'Abdu'l-Bahá has said that He Himself would obey the decisions of the Spiritual Assembly even if He knew that some of those decisions were wrong. Hence, by obeying the Assembly, we are obeying a Command of God.

2.   What should we do if we felt that a decision made by our Local Spiritual Assembly is not correct?

First, we must obey that decision because God has commanded us to do so.   However, we can appeal to the National Spiritual Assembly to reconsider the decision of our Local Spiritual Assembly. By obeying our Local and National Spiritual Assemblies, we strengthen the foundation of Bahá'í Administration. There could be no unity among us if we were each to obey only some of our Assembly's decisions.

3. Can we disobey the decisions of an Assembly because we do not like some of its members?

    No. This is a very bad attitude. Our loyalty to the Spiritual Assembly is not dependent on our liking or disliking its members. It is the institution of Bahá'u'lláh to which we are loyal, no matter who the members of that Assembly may be. The unity of the community is safeguarded only if we lend our complete support to the institutions of the Cause regardless of their members.

4. Can we resign from the membership of a Spiritual Assembly?

    Not unless we have a very good reason, such as continuous bad health or having moved to some other town or village. When we are elected as members of an Assembly, we must remember that God has given us the privilege of serving our community. Our loyalty to the Teachings of Bahá'u'lláh and our love for Him should encourage us to accept any responsibility in the service of His Cause.

5. Can we consult the Spiritual Assembly about our personal problems?

    Yes, we can. 'Abdu'l-Bahá has encouraged the Bahá'ís to take their problems to the Spiritual Assembly and consult them about their difficulties. If, God forbid, there should arise any differences between two Bahá'ís, they should ask the Spiritual Assembly to help them solve their problems, and should willingly accept the decisions of the Assembly.

6. Is the Spiritual Assembly responsible to the Bahá'ís who elect it?

    No. The Local Spiritual Assembly is responsible to God, and in administrative matters to the National Spiritual Assembly of the country. Every Assembly should make decisions based on what is good for the Cause. In problems that may arise between members of the community, the

Assembly should be impartial and just in its decisions. It does not matter how the community may react towards its decisions, so long as the Assembly has been guided by justice.

7. Is the authority of any Bahá'í higher than the authority of a Spiritual Assembly?

No. There is no individual leadership in the Cause. Being Chairman or Secretary of an Assembly does not give an individual any special rights. The Assembly members have no more rights than any other Bahá'í in the community once they leave the Assembly meeting, and like them, have to abide by all the decisions of the Assembly. There is absolute equality of rights in the Bahá'í Faith.

Bahá'í Temples

The Bahá'í Faith is a universal religion. Therefore, the Bahá'í temple is a universal house of worship of God. When Bahá'ís build their temples, they dedicate them to the people of the world. Everyone belonging to any religion, caste or creed is welcome in the Bahá'í temple. The sacred Writings of all religions are read in our temples. People gather in Bahá'í temples as members of one family under one roof to worship one Almighty God.

The structure of the Bahá'í temples is a symbol of unity itself. They are nine-sided buildings. Each side has a door. All these doors open to a central hall under one beautiful dome. These nine doors and the nine-sided structures symbolize the nine major religions of the world. They express the basic unity of all religions. We see only beautiful doors on all sides when we are in the central hall looking around the interior. There is no front or back door in a Bahá'í temple. The doors open on all sides, and all receive light to and send light from the central hall where peoples of all races gather to worship God. This is a wonderful way to show in a building the equality and unity of religions.

The Bahá'í temples are not merely houses of worship. They are institutions. Around these nine-sided temples will be nine humanitarian institutions (such as a school, orphanage, hospital, etc.) each connected to one side of the temple through beautiful roads and pathways. All these roads lead to the House of God. Is this not a beautiful arrangement? It certainly is and it is because 'Abdu'l-Bahá revealed in His Tablets the plan for Bahá'í temples.

At present, there are seven Houses of Worship in seven continents or regions of the world. They are to be found in: Wilmette, near Chicago in the United States of America; Kampala, Uganda; Sydney, Australia; Frankfurt, Germany; New Delhi, India; Panama City, Panama; and Apia, Western Samoa. They are called the mother temples of each continent because in future numerous temples will be built in many countries of the world. The Bahá'ís in many countries have acquired lands to build their temples.[1]

The Bahá'í Fund

Suppose you were living in a village where there was a flood and someone's house had been washed away, leaving him and his children homeless. If you learnt that a number of people were helping to build a shelter for this homeless family, what would you do? Would you say you were too poor to help, or would you come forward to help, no matter how little it might be, to make it possible for this family to have a roof over their heads in the rainy season? You might be able to offer a cartload of stones or a very small sum of money. Your contribution would be one of many other donations that, when combined, would make it possible to build a shelter for this family.

The human race today can be likened to a homeless family caught in the tempest of war and hundreds of other calamities. The Bahá'í Faith is the refuge in which humanity can find peace and happiness. The Bahá'ís of the world are striving to build up

---

1   Sites for future Bahá'í temples exceeds 120.

this shelter for mankind. Would not every one of us come forward to help?

We must establish the institutions of the Cause, build our Centres and Houses of Worship, translate the teachings of the Faith into all the languages of the world, and publish pamphlets and books. To support these and many other undertakings, we need material resources and spiritual help. This is why every Local and National Spiritual Assembly has a special Fund to receive the contributions of the Bahá'ís.

Each contribution must be made voluntarily; no one can oblige us to donate to the funds if we do not wish to do so. However, contributions to our funds are a spiritual obligation, and a test of our faith. No Bahá'í, knowing the importance of this Cause to humanity, can deprive himself of the privilege of helping to raise its institutions and bringing it to the attention of the suffering world.

The amount we give to the Bahá'í Fund is not as important as the spirit in which we give our contribution. 'Abdu'l-Bahá asked the believers of the world to contribute towards the cost of the Temple in the United States when the Bahá'ís there decided to build it. There was an English lady who was very poor but longed to give something for the Temple. All she had in the world that she could sell was her long, beautiful golden hair. Although it meant a great sacrifice, she cut her long hair and contributed the money obtained from selling it to the Fund. In this way she, too, could participate in building a glorious Temple.

Our beloved Guardian said:

"We must be like the fountain or spring that is continually emptying itself of all that it has and is continually being refilled from an invisible source. To be continually giving out for the good of our fellows undeterred by the fear of poverty and reliant on the unfailing bounty of the Source of all wealth and all good—this is the secret of right living."[1]

Every Spiritual Assembly must establish a Fund. Members of the community must contribute according to their capacity by their own free will. By our giving a part of what God has given us, we offer our thanksgiving to our benevolent God.

Remember what 'Abdu'l-Bahá has said:

"O Friends of God! Be ye assured that in place of these contributions, your agriculture, your industry, and your commerce will be blessed by manifold increases, with goodly gifts and bestowals. He who cometh with one goodly deed will receive a tenfold reward. There is no doubt that the living Lord will abundantly confirm those who expend their wealth in His path."[2]

---

1 Shoghi Effendi: *Directives of the Guardian*, No. 83, p. 32.
2 'Abdu'l-Bahá: *Bahá'í Prayers* (US edition), p. 84.

Some of the Laws and Obligations

Cleanliness

Bahá'u'lláh says in the *Book of Aqdas*:

> *"Be ye the very essence of cleanliness amongst mankind."*[1]

> *"Hold ye fast unto refinement under all conditions ...."*[2]

> *"Cleave ye unto the cord of refinement with such tenacity as to allow no trace of dirt to be seen upon your garments."*[3]

> *"Immerse yourselves in clean water; it is not permissible to bathe yourselves in water that hath already been used. ... Truly, We desire to behold you as manifestations of paradise on earth, that there may be diffused from you such fragrance as shall rejoice the hearts of the favoured of God."*[4]

This command of Bahá'u'lláh helps us to understand the importance of cleanliness. God wants us to be healthy and happy throughout our days. If we do not keep clean, our health will suffer. When we are not healthy, then we will not be as happy as we should be.

Science has proved that most of the diseases in the world are caused by uncleanliness. If we eat food with dirty hands, then we endanger our health because many diseases enter our bodies that way. If we put dirty hands on our eyes, we will have eye trouble. In many villages of the world today, people wash their clothes and dishes in water that is not very clean. Sometimes,

---

[1] Bahá'u'lláh: *The Kitáb-i-Aqdas*, para. 74, p. 47.
[2] Bahá'u'lláh: *The Kitáb-i-Aqdas*, para. 46, p. 36.
[3] Bahá'u'lláh: *The Kitáb-i-Aqdas*, para. 74, p. 46.
[4] Bahá'u'lláh: *The Kitáb-i-Aqdas*, para. 106, p. 58.

even their drinking water is polluted, and the diseases and poisoning that it may cause can result in much unhappiness.

Keeping ourselves, our clothes and our homes clean is very important for us as Bahá'ís, not only because we will be healthier and happier, but also because it is a command of Bahá'u'lláh.

'Abdu'l-Bahá has said:

"External cleanliness, although it is but a physical thing, hath a great influence upon spirituality. ... The fact of having a pure and spotless body likewise exercises an influence upon the spirit of man."[1]

Prayer

"If one friend feels love for another he will wish to say so. Though he knows that the friend is aware that he loves him, he will still wish to say so. ... God knows the wishes of all hearts, but the impulse to pray is a natural one, springing from man's love to God ...."[2]

'Abdu'l-Bahá says that *"prayer is conversation with God"*.[3] At another time He says:

"We should speak in the language of heaven—in the language of the spirit—for there is a language of the spirit and heart. It is as different from our language as our own language is different from that of the animals, who express themselves only by cries and sounds.

"It is the language of the spirit which speaks to God. When, in prayer, we are freed from all outward things and turn to

---

1 'Abdu'l-Bahá: *Tablets of 'Abdu'l-Bahá*, Vol. III, pp. 581–82. Second sentence quoted in *The Kitáb-i-Aqdas*, Notes No. 104, p. 212.

2 'Abdu'l-Bahá quoted in J. E. Esselmont: *Bahá'u'lláh and the New Era*, Chapter 6, Prayer the Language of Love section, p. 90. Also given in *The Compilation of Compilations*, (Prayer, Meditation and the Devotional Attitude) Vol. II, No. 1755, p. 236.

3 'Abdu'l-Bahá quoted in J. E. Esselmont: *Bahá'u'lláh and the New Era*, Chapter 6, Conversation with God section, p. 85.

God, then it is as if in our hearts we hear the voice of God.
Without words we speak, we communicate, we converse with
God and hear the answer.... All of us, when we attain to a
truly spiritual condition, can hear the Voice of God. "[1]

Prayer is the food of the soul. We cannot grow strong and
healthy in spirit if we do not pray. Therefore prayer is
compulsory in our religion. Bahá'u'lláh, in His Most Holy Book
(*the Aqdas*), writes:

> *"Recite ye the verses of God every morn and eventide.*
> *Whoso faileth to recite them hath not been faithful to the*
> *Covenant of God and His Testament, and whoso turneth*
> *away from these holy verses in this Day is of those who*
> *throughout eternity have turned away from God. Fear ye*
> *God, O My servants, one and all. Pride not yourselves on*
> *much reading of the verses or on a multitude of pious acts by*
> *night and day; for were a man to read a single verse with joy*
> *and radiance it would be better for him than to read with*
> *lassitude all the Holy Books of God, the Help in Peril, the*
> *Self-Subsisting. Read ye the sacred verses in such measure*
> *that ye be not overcome by languor and despondency. Lay*
> *not upon your souls that which will weary them and weigh*
> *them down, but rather what will lighten and uplift them, so*
> *that they may soar on the wings of the Divine verses towards*
> *the Dawning-place of His manifest signs; this will draw you*
> *nearer to God, did ye but comprehend.* "[2]

From these sacred Words of Bahá'u'lláh we understand that
Bahá'í prayers, though compulsory, must not be treated as a
ritual or ceremony. You will find many people who think that
by the mere recitation of some words, which they usually do not
understand, they are performing a meritorious deed. Some
people believe that if they recite a whole book of Sacred

---

[1]   'Abdu'l-Bahá quoted in J. E. Esselmont: *Bahá'u'lláh and the New Era*,
      Chapter 6, Conversation with God section, pp. 85–86. From a talk reported
      by Miss Ethel J. Rosenberg.
[2]   Bahá'u'lláh: *The Kitáb-i-Aqdas*, para 149, p. 73–74.

Writings in one day, then they will find favour in the sight of God and be rewarded in some manner.

Thousands of people spend hours reading their sacred Books in Sanskrit, Latin or Arabic when they do not understand a word of these languages. They do this because they suppose that the mere recitation of sacred Words will bring them salvation, when in reality they are blindly imitating what their fathers did before them. Lip service worship is not permitted in the Bahá'í Faith.

There are hundreds of beautiful prayers revealed by the Báb, Bahá'u'lláh and 'Abdu'l-Bahá. Bahá'ís are encouraged to read them whenever they wish to pray. Bahá'í meetings usually open and close with prayers. One person reads or chants from the Holy Writings at a meeting while the rest listen and meditate upon the words. The prayers are very inspiring and we can experience great joy and spiritual upliftment when Bahá'í prayers are being recited. These prayers are not obligatory and it is left to every individual to recite them whenever he likes. However, Bahá'ís also have compulsory prayers. Bahá'u'lláh has revealed three such prayers. We are free to select any one of these three prayers, but we must use one of them every day. Of these prayers, there is one that must be said once every 24 hours. It is called the long Obligatory Prayer. Then there is the medium Obligatory Prayer that must be said three times, a day—in the morning, at mid-day and in the evening. The third is the short Obligatory Prayer, to be said once every day at noon.

You can find all these prayers printed in Bahá'í prayer books. The short compulsory prayer can be found in the first chapter of this book under the subject "Purpose of Our Lives" (on page 2). If you decide to say this prayer every noon, it is best to memorize it. However, whichever prayer you choose to say, you must remember that the spirit with which we offer our prayers is of the greatest importance. 'Abdu'l-Bahá says:

"In the highest prayer, men pray only for the love of God, not because they fear Him or hell, or hope for bounty or heaven .... When a man falls in love with a human being, it is

impossible for him to keep from mentioning the name of his beloved. How much more difficult is it to keep from mentioning the Name of God when one has come to love Him .... The spiritual man finds no delight in anything save in commemoration of God."[1]

Fasting

In the Bahá'í Calendar there are four and sometimes five days between the 18th and 19th months of the year that are called the "Days of Há" or the Intercalary Days. During these days Bahá'ís entertain their friends and relatives, or feed the poor amongst them. With the beginning of the 19th month, the month of Loftiness ('Alá), the period of our fasting begins.

Throughout the nineteen days of fasting, we do not eat nor drink anything from sunrise to sunset. We get up at dawn to pray to God and thank Him for all His favours and blessings. Then we eat our food before sunrise and have nothing more during the day until after sunset. We break our fast at sunset after offering our prayers. These 19 days of fasting bring us closer to God than at other times. When we keep the Fast, we are showing in a symbolic way our love for God and our faithfulness in carrying out His commandments.

This is what 'Abdu'l-Bahá says about fasting:

"Fasting is a symbol. Fasting signifies abstinence from lust. Physical fasting is a symbol of that abstinence, and is a reminder; that is, just as a person abstains from physical appetites, he is to abstain from self-appetites and self-desires. But mere abstention from food has no effect on the spirit. It is only a symbol, a reminder. Otherwise it is of no

---

[1] 'Abdu'l-Bahá quoted in J. E. Esselmont: *Bahá'u'lláh and the New Era*, Chapter 6, Prayer the Language of Love section, p. 90 (from notes of Miss Alma Robertson and other pilgrims, November and December 1900). Also quoted in *The Compilation of Compilations*, (Prayer, Meditation and the Devotional Attitude) Vol. II, No. 1756, p. 236; and *Lights of Guidance*, No. 1512, p. 463.

importance. Fasting for this purpose does not mean entire abstinence from food. The golden rule as to food is, do not take too much or too little. Moderation is necessary. There is a sect in India who practise extreme abstinence, and gradually reduce their food until they exist on almost nothing. But their intelligence suffers. A man is not fit to do service for God with brain or body if he is weakened by lack of food. He cannot see clearly.[1]

Before sunrise we prepare ourselves for prayers and meditation. There are beautiful prayers revealed by Bahá'u'lláh especially fox this period. Shortly before sunrise we finish our breakfast. We will not eat or drink from sunrise to sunset. During the period of fasting we, more than ever before, feel our love for Bahá'u'lláh and always remember that it is for His love that we observe the Fast. After sunset we break our fast. We also offer prayers before or after breaking the fast. Though there are a number of prayers especially revealed by Bahá'u'lláh for the fast, we are allowed to offer any one of the revealed prayers from the Bahá'í Holy Books. However, for the convenience of our dear readers, we mention below one of the prayers that may be said during the fasting period:

"Praise be to Thee, O Lord my God! I beseech Thee by this Revelation whereby darkness hath been turned into light, through which the Frequented Fane hath been built, and the Written Tablet revealed, and the Outspread Roll uncovered, to send down upon me and upon them who are in my company that which will enable us to soar into the heavens of Thy transcendent glory, and will wash us from the stain of such doubts as have hindered the suspicious from entering into the tabernacle of Thy unity.

"I am the one, O my Lord, who hath held fast the cord of Thy loving-kindness, and clung to the hem of Thy mercy and

---

1   'Abdu'l-Bahá quoted in J. E. Esselmont: *Bahá'u'lláh and the New Era*, Chapter 11, Fast section, p. 171 (quoted by Miss E. S. Stevens in *Fortnightly Review*, June 1911).

favours. Do Thou ordain for me and for my loved ones the good of this world and of the world to come. Supply them, then, with the Hidden Gift Thou didst ordain for the choicest among Thy creatures.

"These are, O my Lord, the days in which Thou hast bidden Thy servants to observe the fast. Blessed is he that observeth the fast wholly for Thy sake and with absolute detachment from all things except Thee. Assist me and assist them, O my Lord, to obey Thee and to keep Thy precepts. Thou, verily, hast power to do what Thou choosest.

"There is no God but Thee, the All-Knowing, the All-Wise. All praise be to God, the Lord of all worlds."[1]

The period of fasting continues to the last day of the Bahá'í year. New Year's day, which falls on 21 March, marks the end of the fast. Bahá'ís celebrate this day as the Feast of Naw-Rúz.

Work is Worship

One of the laws of Bahá'u'lláh is that everybody should work. It is a sin to beg or to be idle in life and therefore it is forbidden in the Bahá'í Faith. Work is compulsory for everybody in this Cause, and when it is done in the spirit of service to the people of the world, it becomes a form of worship for the Bahá'ís.

Bahá'u'lláh says:

"It is incumbent upon each one of you to engage in some occupation - such as a craft, a trade or the like. We have exalted your engagement in such work to the rank of worship of the one true God. Reflect, O people, on the grace and blessings of your Lord, and yield Him thanks at eventide and dawn."[2]

'Abdu'l-Bahá further explains:

---

[1]   Bahá'u'lláh: *Prayers and Meditations of Bahá'u'lláh*, pp. 9–10.
[2]   Bahá'u'lláh: *The Kitáb-i-Aqdas*, para. 33, p. 30.

"In the Bahá'í Cause arts, sciences and all crafts are (counted as) worship. The man who makes a piece of notepaper to the best of his ability, conscientiously, concentrating all his forces on perfecting it, is giving praise to God. Briefly, all effort and exertion put forth by man from the fullness of his heart is worship, if it is prompted by the highest motives and the will to do service to humanity. This is worship: to serve mankind and to minister to the needs of the people. Service is prayer."[1]

Work is worship! Service is prayer! This is a wonderful law.

When we want to worship God, we must worship Him with happiness and sincerity. Bahá'ís believe that the farmer who is tilling his land for the benefit of himself and others is worshipping God. The carpenter who is making a door for somebody's house, or the tailor who is stitching a garment with all his skill in making it beautiful for someone to enjoy, is giving praise to God.

So we see that, with the blessing of Bahá'u'lláh, every field can become a temple of God, every workshop a house of worship. Therefore, work for a Bahá'í, no matter how difficult or unpleasant it may be, becomes a pleasant occupation because it is a means of worshipping God. Hence a Bahá'í will carry out his work with the same happiness, sincerity and honesty as he performs his prayers.

An ascetic who lives in a cave or in the heart of a jungle is prepared to perform many types of penance because he feels that in doing so he is worshipping God. Bahá'u'lláh has said that the age of asceticism and monkhood has ended. He has, instead, elevated every type of useful work to the level of worshipping God. When we consider it to be a prayer, work can no more be tiresome for us and it will be done with devotion.

---

1   'Abdu'l-Bahá: *Paris Talks*, 176–77.

Renunciation of the world and living a solitary life is not considered meritorious in our Faith. That is why Bahá'ís have no monks nor ascetics among them. Bahá'u'lláh says:

> *"O people of the earth! Living in seclusion or practising asceticism is not acceptable in the presence of God. It behoveth them that are endued with insight and understanding to observe that which will cause joy and radiance. Such practices as are sprung from the loins of idle fancy or are begotten of the womb of superstition ill beseem men of knowledge. In former times and more recently some people have been taking up their abodes in the caves of the mountains while others have repaired to graveyards at night. Say, give ear unto the counsels of this Wronged One. Abandon the things current amongst you and adopt that which the faithful Counsellor biddeth you. Deprive not yourselves of the bounties which have been created for your sake."*[1]

Let us worship God in our fields and our workshops. Let us praise Him by continuous and conscientious work. Let us offer sincere prayers to our creator through our service to mankind. Let us remember this law of God for this age:

> *"Waste not your time in idleness and sloth. Occupy yourselves with that which profiteth yourselves and others. Thus hath it been decreed in this Tablet from whose horizon the day-star of wisdom and utterance shineth resplendent.*
>
> *"The most despised of men in the sight of God are those who sit idly and beg. Hold ye fast unto the cord of material means, placing your whole trust in God, the Provider of all means. When anyone occupieth himself in a craft or trade, such occupation itself is regarded in the estimation of God as an act of worship; and this is naught but a token of His infinite and all-pervasive bounty."*[2]

---

1   Bahá'u'lláh: *Tablets of Bahá'u'lláh*, p. 71.
2   Bahá'u'lláh: *Tablets of Bahá'u'lláh*, p. 26.

Teaching the Cause of God

If anyone asks us what are the duties of a Bahá'í, we can say that a Bahá'í should:

1. Study the Cause
2. Practise its Teachings
3. Spread its Message

Bahá'u'lláh says, *"God hath made it incumbent upon every soul to deliver His Cause according to his ability."*[1]

Why is it necessary for us to teach the Cause of God?

When a person suffers from a terrible disease and then finds a medicine that cures him and brings immediate relief from all his pain and suffering, he will certainly treasure that medicine with great care. Hence, if he sees a friend of his suffering from the same disease, what will he do with the medicine? Will he selfishly keep it for himself and allow his friend to suffer? Of course not! He will gladly give the medicine to his friend and assure him that it will bring immediate relief from his sickness because he has already tested it himself.

Bahá'u'lláh is the All-Knowing Physician, and He has brought a wonderful Medicine that can cure us of all our ailments. The disease of hatred, superstition, despair and disunity is destroying the people of the world. How can a Bahá'í who has himself been cured of these ailments and knows the remedy, be indifferent towards the suffering of others? Surely he must try to share what he himself has received from the teachings of God with his ailing brethren whom he finds in every land.

In the Bahá'í Faith, we have no special people whose job is to preach and spread the Message of God. The responsibility of guiding people to the Cause, therefore, is placed on the shoulders of every individual believer.

---

1 Bahá'u'lláh: *Bahá'í World Faith*, p. 206.

What is our interest in giving the Message of God to others? We are not trying to gather an army. We do not hope for any material gain in giving the Message. We only teach the Cause of God because we feel love towards others and we want them to receive the great bounty that God has bestowed upon us in this age. We should never try to impose our ideas upon other people, nor should we argue with them. If they refuse to accept what we offer them, we will still love them. We never tell people that they are wrong and we are right. We just present the Message that God has sent us through Bahá'u'lláh. It is left to them to accept it. Our love for others is not dependent on their becoming Bahá'ís. This is what Bahá'u'lláh orders us to do:

> *"Defile not your tongues with the cursing and reviling of any soul, and guard your eyes against that which is not seemly. Set forth that which ye possess. If it be favourably received, your end is attained; if not, to protest is vain. Leave that soul to himself and turn unto the Lord, the Protector, the Self-Subsisting. Be not the cause of grief, much less of discord and strife. The hope is cherished that ye may obtain true education in the shelter of the tree of His tender mercies and act in accordance with that which God desireth. Ye are all the leaves of one tree and the drops of one ocean."*[1]

Bahá'u'lláh expects us to teach ourselves before teaching others. This means that we should do our best to learn His teachings and to practice them in our lives before we expect others to follow these teachings. In the Words of Bahá'u'lláh:

> *"It behoveth the people of Bahá to render the Lord victorious through the power of their utterance and to admonish the people by their goodly deeds and character, inasmuch as deeds exert greater influence than words."*[2]

> *The effect of the word spoken by the teacher depends upon his purity of purpose and his severance. Some are content*

---

[1]   Bahá'u'lláh: *Tablets of Bahá'u'lláh*, pp. 27 and 129.
[2]   Bahá'u'lláh: *Tablets of Bahá'u'lláh*, p. 57.

with words, but the truth of words is tested by deeds and dependent upon life. Deeds reveal the station of the man. The words must be according to what has proceeded from the mouth of the Will of God and is recorded in Tablets."[1]

"As to the fundamentals of teaching the Faith: know thou that delivering the Message can be accomplished only through goodly deeds and spiritual attributes, an utterance that is crystal clear and the happiness reflected from the face of that one who is expounding the Teachings. It is essential that the deeds of the teacher should attest the truth of his words. Such is the state of whoso doth spread abroad the sweet savours of God and the quality of him who is sincere in his faith.

"Once the Lord hath enabled thee to attain this condition, be thou assured that He will inspire thee with words of truth, and will cause thee to speak through the breathings of the Holy Spirit."[2]

It is a great privilege for us to become a source of spiritual advancement and blessings to others. There may be nothing more precious for us spiritually than to help people understand the purpose of their lives and for them to become united in one universal Cause. 'Abdu'l-Bahá has said that every Bahá'í should try to guide at least one person to the Cause of Bahá'u'lláh each year.[3] Teaching the Cause of Bahá'u'lláh is not dependent on our education. 'Abdu'l-Bahá says that even if one cannot read and write, he can still prove that he is a true servant of mankind through his deeds and actions.[4] If we live the life of a Bahá'í, people will themselves come to see that we are different because we have put into practice the teachings of God for this age. The

---

1   Bahá'u'lláh quoted in J. E. Esselmont: *Bahá'u'lláh and the New Era*, Chapter 5, Teaching section, p. 77.

2   'Abdu'l-Bahá: *Selections from the Writings of 'Abdu'l-Bahá*, p. 175.

3   'Abdu'l-Bahá: *Selections from the Writings of 'Abdu'l-Bahá*, p. 265.

4   'Abdu'l-Bahá: *The Compilation of Compilations*, Vol. I (Education), p. 282.

importance of teaching the Cause and the blessings it brings us is clearly understood from this Tablet of 'Abdu'l-Bahá:

> *"It is known and clear that today the unseen divine assistance encompasseth those who deliver the Message. And if the work of delivering the Message be neglected, the assistance shall be entirely cut off, for it is impossible that the friends of God could receive assistance unless they be engaged in delivering the Message. Under all conditions the Message must be delivered, but with wisdom. ... The friends should be engaged in educating the souls and should become instruments in aiding the world of humanity to acquire spiritual joy and fragrance. For example: If every one of the friends (believers) were to establish relations of friendship and right dealings with one of the negligent souls, associate and live with him with perfect kindliness, and meanwhile through good conduct and moral behaviour lead him to divine instruction, to heavenly advice and teachings, surely he would gradually arouse that negligent person and would change his ignorance into knowledge."*[1]

Alcoholic Drinks are Prohibited

We have seen how man is distinguished from animals because of his mind and soul. God expects us to take good care of these precious gifts with which He has blessed the human race. We must strive to keep our minds and souls as healthy as possible.

Alcoholic drinks poison the mind to such an extent that people forget their station as human beings and drop to the level of beasts when they are drunk. Therefore, Bahá'u'lláh has forbidden us from using alcoholic drinks altogether.

There are many Bahá'ís who had the habit of using alcoholic drinks before they accepted this Faith. However, after they accepted Bahá'u'lláh as the Manifestation of God for this day, they proved their love and loyalty towards Him by giving up this

---

[1] 'Abdu'l-Bahá: *Tablets of 'Abdu'l-Bahá*, Vol. II, pp. 390–91.

harmful habit that brought nothing but financial, physical and spiritual loss. Now they drink from the water of life that Bahá'u'lláh has provided for us through His teachings, and do not need alcoholic drinks to make them gay or to forget their daily problems.

There are some tribes in the world who were accustomed to serving alcoholic drinks during tribal festivals or ceremonies. They still perform those ceremonies that conform to the Bahá'í laws after becoming Bahá'ís. However, instead of alcoholic drinks, they serve delicious fruit juices that are free from the harm of alcohol.

Use of not only alcohol, but also of drugs not medically prescribed (e.g. opium) that poison the mind and the body (generally those that are habit-forming, mind altering and poisonous), are also forbidden in the Bahá'í Faith.

Observing the Holy Days

There are nine Holy Days each year on which Bahá'ís should not work. These days have been set aside because some special event of great importance in the Cause has taken place on each of them, and hence they are to be treated as special days. Seven of the Holy Days are days of celebration, and two of them commemorate the martyrdom of the Báb and the ascension of Bahá'u'lláh.

The first of the Holy Days is the Feast of Naw-Rúz that marks the end of the fasting period and the beginning of the New Year.

The next three Holy Days occur during the Riḍván festival. This is the anniversary of Bahá'u'lláh's public Declaration that took place in Baghdád. During the twelve days we speak of as "the days of Riḍván", Bahá'u'lláh stayed in a beautiful garden called "Riḍván" where His friends and followers came to see Him for the last time before He was exiled to Constantinople. His many followers, as well as hundreds of other people who had grown to love and respect Him, were filled with grief at His departure. However, the bitter sorrow that weighed the hearts of His lovers was to be changed into eternal joy when they learnt that Bahá'u'lláh was the One Whose coming the Divine Manifestations of the past had foretold, and for whom the Blessed Báb had given His precious life. In memory of those wonderful twelve days, we celebrate the Feast of Ridván every year, and of these days, the first, the ninth and the twelfth are Holy Days on which we do not work.

After Ridván, we have the anniversary of the Declaration of the Báb when the Báb spoke privately of His Mission to Mullá Ḥusayn for the first time in S̲h̲íráz.

The sixth and seventh of our Feast days are the Birthdays of the Báb and Bahá'u'lláh.

Here are the Bahá'í Holy Days:

1	21 March	*Feast of Naw-Rúz (New Year)*
2	21 April	*First day of Riḍván—Declaration of Bahá'u'lláh (1863) at 3 p.m.*
3	29 April	*Ninth day of Riḍván*
4	2 May	*Twelfth day of Riḍván*
5	23 May	*Declaration of the Báb (1844), two hours and eleven minutes after sunset on 22 May*
6	29 May	*Ascension of Bahá'u'lláh (1892) at 3 a.m.*
7	9 July	*Martyrdom of the Báb (1850) at about noon*
8	20 October	*Birthday of the Báb (1819)*
9	12 November	*Birthday of Bahá'u'lláh (1817)*

Sunset is the end of one day and the beginning of another in the Bahá'í calendar. Therefore, each Holy Days starts with the sunset on the previous day. For example, the Declaration of the Báb took place two hours and eleven minutes after sunset on the 22 May and ends at sunset on 23 May. The day of Bahá'u'lláh's ascension starts at sunset on 28 May and ends at sunset on 29 May, etc.

'Abdu'l-Bahá says that we should try to make these Holy Days different from the rest of the days of the year by taking some important step for the progress of the Cause and in service to humanity. We can establish a Bahá'í centre, a Bahá'í class, start a school, or a hospital. Each community will decide what action to take based on its capacity and its special needs. As individuals, too, we can make decisions that will help us to become better Bahá'ís in our personal lives and better members in our community. Hence, according to 'Abdu'l-Bahá, the purpose of a Feast or Holy Day is more than an occasion to eat good food and have a good time. 'Abdu'l-Bahá stated:

> *"As it* [Naw-Rúz] *is a blessed day it should not be neglected or left without results by making it a day limited to the fruits of mere pleasure. During such blessed days institutions should be founded that may be of permanent benefit and value to the people so that in their conversations and in history it may become widely known that such a good work was inaugurated on such a feast day. Therefore, the intelligent must look searchingly into conditions to find out what important affair, what philanthropic institutions are most needed, and what foundations should be laid for the community on that particular day, so that they may be established."*[1]

We do not sit and mourn on the day of the Báb's martyrdom nor Bahá'u'lláh's ascension. Although it is natural for us to feel the grief of these days, we know that the only way to show our loyalty to the Manifestations of God is to dedicate our lives to the service of the Cause for which They lived and died.

Bahá'ís always gather to meet each other and to offer special prayers on the Holy Days. These meetings are very important because through them unity is established among the members of the community, and the unity of the Bahá'ís is a source of divine blessings.

'Abdu'l-Bahá says:

---

1 'Abdu'l-Bahá: Quoted by Baher Forghani in *Days to Remember*, 2nd edn., p. 26.

"... it hath been decided by the desire of God that union and harmony may day by day increase among the friends of God and the maid-servants of the Merciful .... Not until this is realized will the affairs advance by any means whatever! And the greatest means for the union and harmony of all is Spiritual Meetings. This matter is very important and is as a magnet [or to attract] for divine confirmation."[1]

Marriage

We have seen that there is no monastic life in the Bahá'í Faith. Marriage is an important institution in the Bahá'í Faith. In the *Aqdas*, the Most Holy Book, Bahá'u'lláh says:

"Enter into wedlock, O people, that ye may bring forth one who will make mention of Me ...."[2]

'Abdu'l-Bahá says:

"The true marriage of Bahá'ís is this, that husband and wife should be united both physically and spiritually, that they may ever improve the spiritual life of each other, and may enjoy everlasting unity throughout all the worlds of God. This is Bahá'í marriage."[3]

How is the Bahá'í marriage performed? The necessary requirements for a Bahá'í marriage are:

1. The man and woman must consent to marry each other. They cannot be forced to marry each other.
2. Parents of the bride and bridegroom, if alive, must give their consent for the marriage.

Bahá'u'lláh says:

"It hath been laid down in the Bayán[4] *that marriage is dependent upon the consent of both parties. Desiring to*

---

[1] 'Abdu'l-Bahá: *Tablets of 'Abdu'l-Bahá*, Vol. I, pp. 125–26.
[2] Bahá'u'lláh: *The Kitáb-i-Aqdas*, para. 63, p. 42.
[3] 'Abdu'l-Bahá: *Selections from the Writings of 'Abdu'l-Bahá*, p. 118.
[4] The "Mother Book" of the Báb.

establish love, unity and harmony amidst Our servants, We have conditioned it, once the couple's wish is known, upon the permission of their parents, lest enmity and rancour should arise amongst them."[1]

When these necessary consents are obtained, the parties inform their Spiritual Assembly of their intention of getting married and fix a date so that a representative may be sent to witness the marriage. Then in the presence of two witnesses, the bridegroom and the bride will separately repeat the following verse enjoined by Bahá'u'lláh in His Most Holy Book:[2]

'We will all, verily, abide by the Will of God."[3]

The man and the woman then become husband and wife, and the date of the marriage is registered with the Spiritual Assembly.

If there is no Local Spiritual Assembly in the area, the Bahá'í marriage can be performed in the way we have described, by the bride and the bridegroom themselves in the presence of two witnesses. In either case, any additional civil requirements must also be fulfilled.

'Abdu'l-Bahá says:

"But the Bahá'í engagement is the perfect communication and the entire consent of both parties. However, they must show forth the utmost attention and become informed of one another's character and the firm covenant made between each other must become an eternal binding, and their intentions must be everlasting affinity, friendship, unity and life."[4]

In the light of this teaching, marriage is a material and a spiritual union. We are not losing our sons and daughters when

---

1   Bahá'u'lláh: *The Kitáb-i-Aqdas*, para. 65, p. 42.
2   Shoghi Effendi quoted in *Lights of Guidance*, No. 1294, pp. 388–89.
3   Bahá'u'lláh: *The Kitáb-i-Aqdas*, Questions and Answers, No. 3, p. 105.
4   'Abdu'l-Bahá: *Tablets of 'Abdu'l-Bahá*, Vol. II, p. 325.

they get married. We are joining them in a union that also unites their families. It is a customary obligation in some cultures that the bride and her parents (sometimes it is the bridegroom's family) pay a specified sum of money and gifts to the bridegroom's family—a dowry. Disagreements can occur over the value of the dowry and the bride's family sometimes suffers severe financial hardship—especially in poor families or those with many daughters.

The law of Bahá'u'lláh abolishes all previous variations in the dowry and converts it into a symbolic act whereby the bridegroom presents a gift of a certain limited value to the bride. Bahá'u'lláh states:

> *"No marriage may be contracted without payment of a dowry, which hath been fixed for city-dwellers* [the bridegroom] *at nineteen mithqals* [about 69.2 gm] *of pure gold, and for village-dwellers* [the bridegroom] *at the same amount in silver. Whoso wisheth to increase this sum, it is forbidden him to exceed the limit of ninety–five mithqals. Thus hath the command been writ in majesty and power. If he content himself, however, with a payment of the lowest level, it shall be better for him according to the Book."*[1]

There are some beautiful prayers revealed by Bahá'u'lláh and 'Abdu'l-Bahá for marriage[2] that are not obligatory but can be said along with the marriage vow, if so desired.

In marriage, as at any other happy occasion, people of every tribe or nation are free to entertain each other and have any kind of performances that are part of their culture. These customs, however, should not be against the teachings of God in maintaining the purity of character and the dignity of man. There are beautiful folk-dances and folk-songs that enrich the new composite culture of mankind. Bahá'ís are encouraging people to retain their cultural heritage. Therefore, the beautiful

---

1   *Bahá'u'lláh: The Kitáb-i-Aqdas*, para. 66, p. 42.
2   See the Marriage section of the Bahá'í prayer books.

cultural heritage of people, whether relating to marriage or other festive occasions, may be performed.

One may ask if a Bahá'í can marry a non-Bahá'í. A Bahá'í man or woman may marry a non-Bahá'í belonging to any other religion. In fact, one of Bahá'u'lláh's commands is:

"... *to consort with the followers of all religions in a spirit of friendliness and fellowship, to proclaim that which the Speaker on Sinai hath set forth and to observe fairness in all matters.*

"They that are endued with sincerity and faithfulness should associate with all the peoples and kindreds of the earth with joy and radiance, inasmuch as consorting with people hath promoted and will continue to promote unity and concord, which in turn are conducive to the maintenance of order in the world and to the regeneration of nations. Blessed are such as hold fast to the cord of kindliness and tender mercy and are free from animosity and hatred."[1]

A Bahá'í who marries a non-Bahá'í should make it clear to his or her life-partner that he or she is a Bahá'í and must conform to the Bahá'í laws. As a Bahá'í expects his or her non-Bahá'í partner to take part in a simple but dignified Bahá'í ceremony, he or she should also be ready participate in the marriage ceremonies of the religion of his or her partner.

The Bahá'í marriage law is another symbol of the oneness of mankind. It shows that the Bahá'í Faith is not meant for a special cult or group. It is for all mankind.

Loyalty to Government

Bahá'u'lláh has forbidden us to engage in any activity that may harm society. We also have to refrain from anything that is not honest or is subversive. About a hundred years ago Bahá'u'lláh set this principle in one of His Writings:

---

1   Bahá'u'lláh: *Tablets of Bahá'u'lláh*, pp. 35–36.

"In every country where any of this people reside, they must behave towards the government of that country with loyalty, honesty and truthfulness."[1]

A Bahá'í cannot be faithful to his religion if he is not faithful to his government.

'Abdu'l-Bahá has said:

"The essence of the Bahá'í spirit is that, in order to establish a better social order and economic condition, there must be allegiance to the laws and principles of government."[2]

"Furthermore each and every one is required to show obedience, submission and loyalty towards his own government. ... the Baha'is are the well-wishers of the government, obedient to its laws and bearing love towards all peoples."[3]

Loyalty to the government is a part of the character that has to be built up among us. Any act of treachery is a sin. Bahá'u'lláh says:

"Let integrity and uprightness distinguish all thine acts."[4]

"Beautify your tongues, O people, with truthfulness, and adorn your souls with the ornament of honesty. Beware, O people, that ye deal not treacherously with anyone. Be ye the trustees of God amongst His creatures, and the emblems of His generosity amidst His people."[5]

In this connection, another important point may be mentioned that every Bahá'í must observe.

---

1   Bahá'u'lláh: *Tablets of Bahá'u'lláh*, pp. 22–23.
2   'Abdu'l-Bahá: *The Promulgation of Universal Peace*, p. 238.
3   'Abdu'l-Bahá: *Selections from the Writings of 'Abdu'l-Bahá*, p. 239.
4   Bahá'u'lláh: *Epistle to the Son of the Wolf*, p. 93; and *Gleanings from the Writings of Bahá'u'lláh*, CXXX, p. 285.
5   Bahá'u'lláh: *Gleanings from the Writings of Bahá'u'lláh*, CXXXVI, p. 297.

Bahá'ís must avoid any involvement in politics. However, we are still friendly to those who are involved in politics. We believe that God has set a direction for us to spend our energies and resources in building up a divine World Order. We have a plan given to us by God that includes all the good points of the existing political parties and much more, without their shortcomings.

God has set a straight path for us to tread. This path is neither inclined towards left nor right, neither to the East nor the West. It is the path that will lead to the unity of all mankind, regardless of their nationality, creed or social class. Moreover, the Order that Bahá'u'lláh has established in the world is divine in origin and necessarily is quite different in nature, scope and dimension from that of the existing man-made, and often conflicting, ideologies.

There is another reason that a Bahá'í cannot participate in political movements. This has been explained by Shoghi Effendi, the Guardian, in one of his letters:

"We Bahá'ís are one the world-over, we are seeking to build up a new World Order, Divine in origin. How can we do this if every Bahá'í is a member of a different political party— some of them diametrically opposed to each other? Where is our unity then? We would be divided because of politics, against ourselves, and this is the opposite of our purpose. Obviously if one Bahá'í in Austria is given freedom to choose a political party and join it, however good its aims may be, another Bahá'í in Japan, or America or India, has the right to do the same thing, and he might belong to a party the very opposite in principle to that which the Austrian Bahá'í belongs to. Where would be the unity of the Faith then? These two spiritual brothers would be working against each other, because of their political affiliations (as the Christians of Europe have been doing in so many fratricidal wars).

"The best way for a Bahá'í to serve his country and the world is to work for the establishment of Bahá'u'lláh's

World Order, which will gradually unite all men and do away with divisive political systems and religious creeds. "[1]

How One Becomes a Bahá'í

Many times we hear this question: "How can I become a Bahá'í?"

Some people think that the Bahá'í Faith is a society that invites members. This is not correct. Some other people think that Bahá'ís require people to change their names and to give them a new denomination in religious spheres. This also is not correct.

Becoming a Bahá'í means you are convinced of the Oneness of God, the oneness of religions and the oneness of mankind; you realize that religion is progressive and continuous; and that religion aims for unity rather than disunity. A Bahá'í, moreover, is convinced that all religions are divine in origin and are equal. However, a Bahá'í believes that Bahá'u'lláh (the Glory of God) is the Manifestation of God for this age. Additionally, Bahá'u'lláh, like the Manifestations of God in the past, has come to open a new era of happiness and unity for us in this age. When one becomes a Bahá'í, he finds the love of Bahá'u'lláh in his heart. When this conviction is there, we are Bahá'ís. No ceremony, baptism nor change of name is necessary to enrol a person into the Bahá'í Faith. In other words, any conversion results from an individual's own inner conviction and does not need to be validated by a ceremony.

'Abdu'l-Bahá says:

'The man who lives the life according to the teachings of Bahá'u'lláh is already a Bahá'í. "[2]

---

1   Shoghi Effendi: *Light of Divine Guidance*, Vol. I, pp. 123–24. (Letter on behalf of Shoghi Effendi dated 24 June 1947)
2   'Abdu'l-Bahá quoted in J. E. Esselmont: *Bahá'u'lláh and the New Era*, Chapter 5, Living the Life section, p. 69.

The aims of the Bahá'ís are to serve men and to bring unity and happiness to the world. Bahá'ís are trying to change the hearts of men. The change of heart is not possible except by the power of the Words of God.

'Abdu'l-Bahá was once asked, *"What is a Bahá'í?"* He replied that *"To be a Bahá'í simply means to love all the world; to love humanity and try to serve it; to work for universal peace and universal brotherhood."*[1]

"If he is a Bahá'í in reality, his deeds and actions will be decisive proofs of it. What are the requirements? Love for mankind, sincerity toward all, reflecting the oneness of the world of humanity, philanthropy, becoming enkindled with the fire of the love of God, attainment to the knowledge of God and that which is conducive to human welfare."[2]

When a mirror is clean, it reflects the light. When it is not clean, it does not reflect anything. If Bahá'ís teach their religion to others, it is an attempt to clean the dust of prejudice, hatred and animosity from the mirrors of human hearts. When pure-hearted people meet the Sun of Truth, they receive the light in great measure and reflect it to others.

Many Bahá'ís of today are those who had always felt in their hearts the necessity of having new teachings for this new age, but they did not know how they could realize their feelings in practice. They did not know that there was a religion in the world that contained all the teachings they wished to exist in a religion. When they heard about the Bahá'í Faith, they believed in it as the Voice of God because they had already heard the Voice of God in their hearts without knowing about Bahá'u'lláh. They are those clean mirrors that have now been aimed towards the rays of the Sun of Truth and reflect its splendour. The

---

[1] 'Abdu'l-Bahá quoted in J. E. Esselmont: *Bahá'u'lláh and the New Era*, Chapter 5, Living the Life section, p. 69.

[2] 'Abdu'l-Bahá: *The Promulgation of Universal Peace*, p. 336.

mirrors of hearts, though clean, will remain dark if they are not turned towards the light.

You become a Bahá'í when this conviction and realization of truth occurs. However, there is a form to be filled in and signed by the Bahá'ís, giving their names and addresses, to inform the National Spiritual Assembly of their country that they believe in Bahá'u'lláh. In this way you inform the Bahá'í world community that you are a fellow believer in Bahá'u'lláh. You become a member of that community when the signed declaration form is accepted. By signing the declaration form, you pledge yourself to serve humanity through the God-given administration that is a part of the divine guidance for this age. Declaration forms are issued by the National Spiritual Assembly of each country and are given to the believers in Bahá'u'lláh in that country to sign. The signed forms are returned to the National Assembly through the Local Spiritual Assemblies. Where there is no Local Assembly, those who declare themselves as Bahá'ís may send the form directly to the National Spiritual Assembly.

Being a member of the Bahá'í community is not the same as joining a club. Bahá'ís have been given God's plan for the uniting of humanity and, as members of the community, we are working together to implement that plan in the manner most suited to our capabilities and experience. This means our individual efforts are co-ordinated rather than regimented. Membership of the Bahá'í Faith gives us the right and the responsibility to take an active part in the process of uniting mankind. Membership in other religions differs in that the responsibility and direction of actions are left to their religious leaders. In the past, religion has been concerned with the spiritualization of individuals; whereas in the Bahá'í Faith, this has been extended to include the spiritualization of mankind. Individuals loving the Bahá'í principles, but working as individuals, will each go in their own direction without the guidance of a common God-directed goal.

A Bahá'í serves men and prays for them. Among the innumerable beautiful prayers revealed, we read:

"O Thou kind Lord! Thou hast created all humanity from the same stock. Thou hast decreed that all shall belong to the same household. In Thy Holy Presence they are all Thy servants, and all mankind are sheltered beneath Thy Tabernacle; all have gathered together at Thy Table of Bounty; all are illumined through the light of Thy Providence.

"O God! Thou art kind to all, Thou hast provided for all, dost shelter all, conferrest life upon all. Thou hast endowed each and all with talents and faculties, and all are submerged in the Ocean of Thy Mercy.

"O Thou kind Lord! Unite all. Let the religions agree and make the nations one, so that they may see each other as one family and the whole earth as one home. May they live together in perfect harmony.

"O God! Raise aloft the banner of the oneness of mankind.
"O God! Establish the Most Great Peace.
"Cement Thou, O God, the hearts together.

"O Thou kind Father, God! Gladden our hearts through the fragrance of Thy love. Brighten our eyes through the Light of Thy Guidance. Delight our ears with the melody of Thy Word, and shelter us all in the Stronghold of Thy Providence.

"Thou art the Mighty and Powerful, Thou art the Forgiving and Thou art the One Who overlooketh the shortcomings of all mankind."[1]

---

[1] 'Abdu'l-Bahá: *The Promulgation of Universal Peace*, p. 100.